THE AMERICANS

THE AMERICANS

EDWIN DAVIES SCHOONMAKER

ISBN: 978-93-90145-02-7

Published: 1913

LECTOR HOUSE LLP
E-MAIL: lectorpublishing@gmail.com

THE AMERICANS

BY

EDWIN DAVIES SCHOONMAKER

1913

TO
MY FATHER AND MY BROTHER FRANK

AUTHOR'S NOTE

The drama here published is logically the third in a series of racial dramas, as follows:

1. *The Saxons*
2. *The Slavs*
3. *The Americans*
4. *The Hindoos*

Of this series *The Saxons*, dealing with man's struggle for religious liberty, has already been published. For reasons that need not be given, it has been thought best to postpone *The Slavs*, which will present man's battle for political liberty, and offer *The Americans*, the theme of which is the industrial conflict that is now raging. *The Hindoos*, a drama of spiritual unfoldment, will come in its order.

CONTENTS

PERSONS OF THE DRAMA

J. Donald Egerton	Lumber king and mill-owner
Augustus Jergens	A partner
Sam Williams	Leader of the strikers
General Chadbourne	In command of the State Militia
Captain Haskell	Second in command
Rev. Ezra Hardbrooke	Bishop of the Diocese
John. W. Braddock	Governor of the State
Ralph Ardsley	Editor of the Foreston Courier
Chief of Police	Coöperating with the Militia
George Egerton	Son of Donald Egerton
Harry Egerton	Son of Donald Egerton
Harvey Anderson	Former cowboy and Rough Rider
Buck Bentley	One of the Militia
Wes Dicey	A walking delegate
Jim King	Supporter of Dicey
Rome Masters	Supporter of Dicey
Cap Saunders	An old miner
Bill Patten	Striker, off in search of work
Silas Maury	Striker, off in search of work
Willie Maury	Son of Silas Maury
Mary Egerton	Wife of Donald Egerton
Gladys Egerton	Daughter of Donald Egerton
Sylvia Orr	Friend of Mrs. Egerton

A chauffeur, a butler, a doctor, a nurse, two maids, two detectives, two sentries, strikers, strike-breakers, militiamen, guests at the reception, etc.

A land is not its timber but its people,
And not its Art, my father, but its men.

—Harry Egerton.

THE AMERICANS

ACT I

THE MINE

Scene: On the mountains in a timber region of north-western America. In every direction, as far as the eye can see, a wilderness of stumps with piles of brush black with age and sinking from sheer rottenness into the ground. Here and there a dead pine stands up high against the horizon. In the distance, left, cleaving the range and extending on back under an horizon of cold gray clouds, is seen the line of a river of which this whole region is apparently the watershed, for everywhere the land slopes toward it. In the remote distance, beyond the river, innumerable bare buttes, and beyond these a gray stretch of plains. Down the mountains, left, six or seven miles away, the river loops in and a portion of a town is seen upon its banks. At this end of the town, upon a hill overlooking the river, a large white mansion conspicuous for the timber about it. At the farther end, a huge red saw-mill occupies the centre of a vast field of yellow lumber piles, the tall black stack of the mill clearly outlined against the gray of the land beyond.

Back, a hundred yards or so, a road, evidently constructed years ago when the logs were being taken out, comes up on the flats from the direction of the town, turns sharply to the right and goes toward the ridge. Beyond this road, just at the curve, standing out among the stumps, an old stationary engine eaten up with rust and an abandoned logging-wagon, the hind part resting upon the ground, the two heavy wheels lying upon it. Farther back a small cabin falling into decay. Here and there patches of creeping vines and rank grass cover the ground, hiding in some places to a considerable depth the bases of the stumps. But to the left, where it is evident a steep slope plunges down, and also in the foreground, are open spaces with boulders and, scattered about under a thin loam of rotted needles and black cones, the outlines of a few flat stones. In the immediate foreground, left, a huge boulder, weighing possibly four or five tons, barely hangs upon the slope, ready at any moment, one would think, to slip and plunge down.

Two men, Cap Saunders and Harvey Anderson, the latter down left, the former to the right and farther back, are slowly coming forward. Each has a camping outfit, a roll of blankets, etc., upon his back, and carries in his hands a plaster cast of what would seem to be a cross-section of a log. It is about two feet in diameter and three inches thick. As they come along they try the casts on the various stumps and carefully turn them about to see if they fit, then chip the stump with a hatchet to indicate that it has been tried.

Time: The evening of a day early in November in the present time.

HARVEY ANDERSON.

    And say two dollars profit on each log.

CAP SAUNDERS.

    That's low enough.

HARVEY ANDERSON.

    Suppose a man could walk
    Over the mountains with a great big sack
    And pick two silver dollars from each stump.
    It's forty miles to where the trees begin,
    And on each side the river eight or ten.
    Think what he'd have.

CAP SAUNDERS.

    He's made work for them, Harvey.

HARVEY ANDERSON.

    Have millions, wouldn't he?

Cap Saunders.

    I suppose he would.
    But where would this land be? There'd be no homes.
    And what are forests for but to cut down?

HARVEY ANDERSON.

    You wouldn't hear him say, 'Now, Harvey, you
    Go in and get your sack full; I'll stay out';
    Or 'Now it's your turn, Cap.' Not on your life.
    He'd walk his legs off, but he'd have them all.
    Or what's more likely, he'd let others walk,
    And send his wagons out and get the sacks
    And have them brought in to him.

CAP SAUNDERS.

    For myself
    I'd rather be out here though on the mountains
    Than live in his big mansion.

HARVEY ANDERSON.

    So would I.
    But that don't mean I'd rather tramp the flats
    Picking up dollars for some other man.
    And I suppose the mill-boys feel the same.

CAP SAUNDERS.

> A fellow has to do the best he can.
> If he can stake himself, then off, I say,
> And pan for his own self. That's been my way.
> Sometimes I've struck pay dirt and sometimes not.
> And then I'd go and dig for a month or two
> For the other boys until I'd got my stake— —

HARVEY ANDERSON.

> Here is another like the one back there;
> Goes half way round as clean as anything;
> And the bark seems the same; but on this side— —

CAP SAUNDERS.

> *(Who has left his cast and is hurrying forward excitedly)*

> Hold her a minute!

HARVEY ANDERSON.

> No, it don't fit, Cap.
> The same old finger width it's always been.
> When the curve matches, then there's some damn knot;
> And when the knot's not there, it's something else.
> No, you can't stretch it. Now it's this side; see?
> 'Twas best the way I had it. There you are.
> Might as well mark her.

CAP SAUNDERS.

> It's a close miss, sure.
> It's like the one I found upon the ridge
> Week before last.

HARVEY ANDERSON.

> The place where it don't match
> Is always on the side that you don't see
> Until your heart's jumped up.

> *(Chips the stump)*

> That ends the day.

CAP SAUNDERS.

> I think I'll work a while.

> *(Starts back)*

HARVEY ANDERSON.

> The sun's gone down.

CAP SAUNDERS.

I haven't heard the whistle of the mill.

HARVEY ANDERSON.

Nor like to.

CAP SAUNDERS.

Ah! I keep forgetting that.
When a man's heard her blow for years and years
He can't be always thinking that she's stopped.
I wonder how the strike is getting on.

HARVEY ANDERSON.

As everything gets on that's Egerton's.
He'll cut them down as he's cut down the trees.

*(Sits upon a stump and looks off up the valley, then turns and watches
the old man busy with his cast)*

HARVEY ANDERSON.

Your old bones must be tired, Cap.

CAP SAUNDERS.

How so?

HARVEY ANDERSON.

How long have you been hunting for this thing?

CAP SAUNDERS.

Before this search, you mean?

HARVEY ANDERSON.

Yes.

CAP SAUNDERS.

Off and on,
Thirty or forty years.

HARVEY ANDERSON.

And won't give up?

CAP SAUNDERS.

Not till I'm dead.

HARVEY ANDERSON.

You ought to have been an ox.

You've got the wrong form, Cap. You think you'd be
As patient if the prize was for yourself?

CAP SAUNDERS.

When one's been on a trail for years and years
It ain't the game he cares for; it's the chase.
And like as not when he's brought down the buck
He'll leave the carcass lying on the rocks,
Taking a piece or two, then off again.
As for what's done with it, I don't care that.
But I would like to know where that tree stood.

HARVEY ANDERSON.

And you think the boys down there should be the same,
The boys that saw the dollars from the logs,
Sacking the silver up, be satisfied
To have him take the silver, leaving them
The bark on either side?

CAP SAUNDERS.

I don't say that.

HARVEY ANDERSON.

Give me the carcass when you find it, Cap,
And you can have the chase. I'd like to know
For one time in my life just how it feels
To have your pockets full and taste the towns.
And I think the boys that saw the logs down there
Are more like me, Cap, than they are like you.

(Picks up his cast and comes forward)

CAP SAUNDERS.

Egerton ain't a-holdin' them. They can go
If they ain't satisfied.

HARVEY ANDERSON.

Yes, they can go.
They're like the red men, they can always go.

*(In an open space in the foreground he puts his things down upon the
ground. He goes right to a pile of brush, pulls out a black limb, and
proceeds to break it across his knee, throwing the pieces in a little heap
upon the ground)*

They've got a Mayor down there, I suppose.
What if he said, 'If you don't like my way,
If you ain't satisfied, there's the road off there?'

Or say the lad we've got in Washington—
What if he said, 'If you don't like my way,
There's ships there in the harbor?' Think we'd leave?
You've had your eyes, Cap, on the ground so long
That you've forgotten there's such things as men.

*(The old man comes down to the stump which he and Anderson tried
earlier in the scene. Anderson picks up his kindling and goes left and
proceeds to start a fire. The night gathers quickly)*

CAP SAUNDERS.

(Trying the stump)

Be careful, Harvey, or they'll see the flame
And think it's found already.

HARVEY ANDERSON.

I don't care.
'Twould serve them right.

CAP SAUNDERS.

They're watching at this hour.

HARVEY ANDERSON.

'Now we've got millions!' then say 'April Fool.'
God, I don't blame them though; I'd do it too.

*(Picks up a blanket and, sticking pieces of brush in the ground, hangs it
between the fire and the town)*

CAP SAUNDERS.

Aug. Jergens he'd be mighty mad, I tell you.

HARVEY ANDERSON.

If I could put men out, you bet I would.
And when I found the gold I'd make her fly.
You wouldn't catch me quarrelling with a lot
Of fellows for the bones, I tell you that.
I'd take a rump or two, then say, 'Light in
And fill your bellies'; or, 'Come on; I'm rich;
Let's take a turn together.' And I'd buy
A train or two and we'd all take a spin
Around the world. I'd make their hair stand up.
I'd show those eastern fellows once or twice.

(Goes left and climbs up on the boulder and looks back over the waste)

CAP SAUNDERS.

(*Coming forward*)

You'll have that rolling down if you don't mind.

HARVEY ANDERSON.

And that's one reason I'll be always broke,
For I know how to spend, while Egerton
And Jergens and those fellows down there don't,
In spite of their big houses. They know how
To quarrel with men and squeeze their last dime out,
But they don't know how to say, 'By God, come on;
Let's have a drink together; we're all friends.'

(*The old man busies himself about the fire, preparing the evening meal.
Anderson sits down on the boulder and looks off up the valley. Where
the town was seen, lights begin to appear*)

HARVEY ANDERSON.

You'll wake up some day, Cap, and look about
And Harvey will be gone.

CAP SAUNDERS.

You don't mean that!
You ain't took no offence at what I said?

HARVEY ANDERSON.

Mad as the Devil, Cap.

CAP SAUNDERS.

Don't you know, Harvey,
About the rolling stone?

HARVEY ANDERSON.

There's some stones, Cap,
Would rather have the motion than the moss.

CAP SAUNDERS.

You're sure a wild one, Harvey; that you are.
You'd stir a muss up, that's what you would do.

(*Goes to the boulder and stands beside Anderson, and they both look off
up the valley*)

HARVEY ANDERSON.

The mansion all lit up—what's going on?

(*They are silent*)

It's a strange world, Cap, it's a funny world.

You throw a piece of bread down; it draws ants,
Red ants and black ants, little ants and big,
And if you'll keep it up you'll have them here
Building their hills about you; you know that.

CAP SAUNDERS.

> (*Returning to the fire*)

It's wonderful how much some men can do.

HARVEY ANDERSON.

Well, men are ants, and Egerton he's had bread.
And he's kept throwing it down there in the valley,
First crumb by crumb and later chunk by chunk,
Until he's drawn them round him, thousands of them,
And when they've come he's put them all to work.
And to see them at it! I could spend my life
Sitting upon the mountains on some rock
That hangs above the town, watching them drudge.
'Get me my logs out;' and they get his logs.
'Now saw them; make me lumber;' and they do it,
'Build me my railroad;' and they blast the rocks.
'Now up with my big mansion on the hill,
And carve me all my ants upon the walls,
Some sawing logs, others with axes raised
Hard at the big round boles, some half cut down;
Make her look like a forest through and through.'
And they've tugged at it till they've got it done.
And all they've chopped and sawed and built is his,
And he puts it in his pocket and sits down
And they can't help themselves. They've got to eat,
And Egerton he's the man that's— —

> (*He has risen and stands looking back through the darkness*)

CAP SAUNDERS.

What do you say,
Harvey, let's spend the night back in the cabin.
It ain't the cold I mind, but from the air
I wouldn't be surprised if it would snow.

HARVEY ANDERSON.

By God, Cap!

CAP SAUNDERS.

Eh?

Harvey Anderson.

Looks like the boys had found it.

Cap Saunders.

You don't, don't say!

(Goes to the boulder)

Harvey Anderson.

Off there, beyond the knob.

(Bill Patten comes through the darkness, rear right. He looks about,
then spies the men)

Bill Patten.

You got some grub that you can spare, boys?

(Goes near the men and gets their line of vision)

That?
It's the moon rising.

Cap Saunders.

Ah, I'm glad, I'm glad!

Harvey Anderson.

Against the sky it looked like some far fire.

(Gets down from the boulder)

Bill Patten.

You're of the force that's huntin' for the mine?

Harvey Anderson.

That's 'hunting' for it, yes.

Bill Patten.

You'll find it.

Harvey Anderson.

Why?

Bill Patten.

Egerton's luck.

(Calls back)

O Silas!

(To Anderson)

'Tain't no use
A-fightin' that old wolf or 'spectin' God
To put his hand between J. D. and gold.
He's got a devil that takes care of him.

(Silas Maury and his son Willie, a boy of twelve or thirteen, enter rear)

BILL PATTEN.

And the same devil blacks Aug. Jergens' boots.
I'd like to get that man in some lone spot.

(They sit down. The workmen seize food and eat ravenously)

HARVEY ANDERSON.

Mill-hands?

(Patten nods)

How's the strike?

BILL PATTEN.

I ain't a man
To show the white while there's a chance to win.

SILAS MAURY.

They've got till sun-down to report for work.

BILL PATTEN.

They'll feel like dogs, too, goin' in that gate,
After the bluff they've made, lickin' his hand.
Me for some other town. I'd rather starve.

SILAS MAURY.

They're 'ranging to bring in a lot of scabs
To-morrow, when the Governor will be there.

BILL PATTEN.

Much as to say, 'Now knock 'em!' Son of a bitch!

HARVEY ANDERSON.

The Governor?

CAP SAUNDERS.

What's the trouble?

BILL PATTEN.

Cakes and pies.

SILAS MAURY.

It's Egerton's big reception.

HARVEY ANDERSON.

(*To Cap Saunders*)

Explains the lights.
They're getting things in shape.

SILAS MAURY.

Yes.

(*He and Anderson walk a little way left and look back toward the mansion*)

BILL PATTEN.

When the boys
First talked of strikin' when they made the cut
I said, 'Don't do it. Egerton's a man—
You'd better fight the Devil than fight him.
He'll show no mercy on you if you cross him.'
I guess they know by now that Bill was right.
Sam Williams though he thinks he knows. 'Hang on.'
All right, hang on; but you will see what comes.
It's hell. I'd rather die out on some rock.

SILAS MAURY.

There ain't no room for poor men in this world.
I don't know what God ever made us for.

(*He and Anderson return to the fire*)

BILL PATTEN.

The man that's got no home's a lucky man.

SILAS MAURY.

I said to Willie, 'I'm glad mother's dead.'

(*A pause*)

WILLIE MAURY.

Think she can see us, pa?

SILAS MAURY.

I don't think so.

BILL PATTEN.

She's better off.

Silas Maury.

> That's true. I hope she can't.
> She died a-thinkin' Willie would be rich
> Some day, if they ever found the mine.

Bill Patten.

> (*Bitterly*)
>
> Give 'em your apples and expect the core.

Silas Maury.

> It came so quick, though, Bill; he didn't think.

Bill Patten.

> If he had just kept still and called to Chris
> And had him help and roll the log aside
> And then at night let some of us men know,
> We could have slipped it out and hidden it,
> And gone to Egerton and said, 'See here,
> We've found the log that you've been lookin' for
> These years and haven't found it— —'

Cap Saunders.

> You don't mean— —

Bill Patten.

> 'And if you'll do the square thing we'll cough up;
> If not, we'll go and find the mine ourselves.'

Cap Saunders.

> You don't mean 'twas the boy that found the log!

Silas Maury.

> Willie here found it.

Cap Saunders.

> Well, well, well! H-u-rrah!
> Hurrah, I say!
>
> (*Throws his hat into the air. Harry Egerton comes through the dark-*
> *ness rear right*)

Cap Saunders.

> If I could call the men,
> Call up the men, my son, who've spent their lives
> Tryin' to get a peep of that there trunk—

You hear that, boys, you up there in the air?

BILL PATTEN.

He'd come to terms, all right, you bet your life.

HARRY EGERTON.

Good evening, men. I'm turned around a bit,
Or seem to be. Just where is Foreston?

HARVEY ANDERSON.

You see those lights down there?

(*He walks back, left. Harry Egerton joins him, going across rear*)

HARRY EGERTON.

That's east?

HARVEY ANDERSON.

Correct.

HARRY EGERTON.

And how far am I from it?

HARVEY ANDERSON.

About six miles.

HARRY EGERTON.

From Foreston, I mean?

HARVEY ANDERSON.

Six miles or more.

HARRY EGERTON.

So far!

(*He walks back a little way, then stops and looks off up the valley.
Harvey Anderson comes forward and begins to break some brush to
replenish the fire*)

CAP SAUNDERS.

Who is it, Harvey?

HARVEY ANDERSON.

I don't know.

CAP SAUNDERS.

And it had the sign cut in the bark, eh?

SILAS MAURY.

Yes.

WILLIE MAURY.

Two X's and a spade.

CAP SAUNDERS.

That's it, that's it!
'Two X's and a spade, then dig nine feet.'
There's two bits, son. How did it happen, dad?

SILAS MAURY.

It came up into the mill with the other logs,
Lookin' just like 'em, but Willie spied the sign—

WILLIE MAURY.

Just as it was goin' into the saws.

SILAS MAURY.

And shouted to Chris Knudson. Chris shut down;
There was a crowd; and then Aug. Jergens come
And had it hauled away.

CAP SAUNDERS.

If you and me
Had been out here, son, when all these were trees
And you'd a-spied that sign, I tell you what,
I'd hung some nuggets round this little neck.

HARVEY ANDERSON.

You'd better wait until the moon comes out.
It's a rough road back there.

HARRY EGERTON.

There is a road?

HARVEY ANDERSON.

A logging road.

HARRY EGERTON.

    (*Coming forward, notices the casts upon the ground*)
You're searching for the mine?

HARVEY ANDERSON.

Cap and I here. These men are from the mill.

Harry Egerton.

(*With interest*)

From the mill down in Foreston, you mean?

Harvey Anderson.

Leaving in search of work.

Harry Egerton.

Are things so bad
Down at the mill, my friends, that you must leave?
Are others leaving? Have the men gone back?

(*The men glare at him*)

Cap Saunders.

They'll have to soon, they say; their grub's give out.

Harvey Anderson.

The Company has given them till to-morrow night
To come to work or be shut out for good.

Harry Egerton.

Have they brought in more men?

Harvey Anderson.

They're arranging to.

Harry Egerton.

I do not see, friends, what you hope to gain
By leaving Foreston and wandering off
In search of work. In the first place I know,
As you perhaps do not, that Egerton
Has given orders to the neighboring plants
To take on no more men until this strike
Is settled, till it's won. And, as you know,
For forty miles around the mills are his,
The camps are his. And where his power ends,
Others begin that work in harmony
With Egerton and Company. They are one,
And have an understanding in some things
Far more than you suspect.

(*Patten and Maury rise and walk aside and whisper together*)

And they all know
Whatever be the outcome of this strike
The effect of it will reach them all at last.

If you men win, mill-workers everywhere
Will take new heart and stand for better things.
But if the Company wins, others will say—
And with no little weight—'We cannot pay
The present scale of wages and compete
With Egerton and Company.' So it will go
Until the farthest mill in all this land
Puts in its hand and takes a ten per cent
Out of the wages of its workingmen.
And there's no power on earth that can prevent it.

(Willie Maury rises and joins his father and Patten)

But even were this not true, were places open,
The same conditions would confront you there
As now confront you here. At any time
Those who employ you have you in their power
And can reduce your wages when they choose,
Lay on you what conditions they see fit,
And you must either yield or be turned forth
To wander on again. I do not know
Whether you men have families or not,
But others have, and their cause is your own.
You cannot wander on for evermore,
Picking up here and there a chance day's work
And hoping that to-morrow things will change,
For changes do not come except through men.

(The men return to the fire)

And so I do not see just what it is
You hope to gain by leaving Foreston.
You cannot spend your lives on highways, friends.
Where will you go? Have you some place in mind?

BILL PATTEN.

It's none of your damn business where we go.
We don't wear no man's collar.

SILAS MAURY.

Bill is right.

BILL PATTEN.

Nor Egerton's, nor no man's on this earth.

HARRY EGERTON.

I beg your pardon, friends, I did not mean——

BILL PATTEN.

We're twenty-one years old and we're free men.

HARRY EGERTON.

I did not mean you had no right to go.
You have.

BILL PATTEN.

You bet we have.

SILAS MAURY.

You can't get men
And want to scare us back, that's what you want,
Talkin' as how the mills will shut us out.

HARRY EGERTON.

I have no wish to scare you back, my friend.

BILL PATTEN.

Then what's your proposition?

HARRY EGERTON.

I have none.

BILL PATTEN.

Come up to shake hands, eh, and say, Good-bye?

HARRY EGERTON.

I chanced upon you here.

BILL PATTEN.

'Chanced' hell! We know.

SILAS MAURY.

If it's my rent you're after, if it's that,
I think you might at least let that much go
For what my boy did, findin' of the log.

HARRY EGERTON.

Friends, you misunderstand me if you think
That I am here to speak for any man,
Or round you up, or lift one hand to stay
Your coming or your going. You are free
And can do what you please.

BILL PATTEN.

You bet we can,
For all your bayonets.

HARRY EGERTON.

My bayonets?

BILL PATTEN.

Yes.

SILAS MAURY.

Think we don't know you, eh?

HARRY EGERTON.

I do not know,
I do not know what I can say to you.
I understand just how you— —

SILAS MAURY.

(*Plucks him by the sleeve and points off up the valley*)

There's your home,
Off there in that big mansion on the hill.
Go there and live your life; you're none of us.

HARRY EGERTON.

My father is my father; I am I.

(*The men prepare to leave. Cap Saunders rises and begins to pack up the things*)

HARRY EGERTON.

We do not choose the gates through which we come
Into this world, my friends. Nor you nor I
Selected who should cradle us nor what home
Should give us shelter. 'Tis what we do that counts,
Not whence we come. Do not misjudge me, friends.
Because I am a son of Egerton
Deny me not the right to be a man.

SILAS MAURY.

You wear our sweat in your fine clothes all right.

HARRY EGERTON.

I wear, my friend, what my own hands have earned.
Where will you go?

SILAS MAURY.

We'll go where we can find— —

BILL PATTEN.

Don't tell him, Si. Don't you see through his game?
Keeps askin' where we're goin'. Don't you see?
He's a spy of the Company.

HARRY EGERTON.

Ah, you do not know
Why I am here. God knows I did not come— —

WILLIE MAURY.

Thought we wouldn't know him.

SILAS MAURY.

Poor men are fools.

WILLIE MAURY.

He's been
Doggin' our footsteps.

BILL PATTEN.

You've been followin' us
To find out where— —

CAP SAUNDERS.

Don't quarrel, men.

BILL PATTEN.

It's a good thing
Your old man crushed me till I pawned my gun,
Or, God, I'd kill you. Do you understand?

HARRY EGERTON.

Hold on there, pard.

BILL PATTEN.

So he could have the mills
Blacklist us. Curse you! And curse all your kind!
You've ground us down until we're dogs, damn you.

SILAS MAURY.

Come sneakin' round to— —

HARRY EGERTON.

Friend, I did not come
To spy on any man or seek you out
Here on the mountains. For my hope has been — —

BILL PATTEN.

We'll blow you up some day, you mark my word.

HARRY EGERTON.

That never one of you would leave the ranks
In your great struggle in the valley there,
But that you would stand fast, and somehow win
In spite of everything, starvation, death.
And I have done all that I could to help you.
But you, my friends, O you must understand,
As there are some things that you cannot do,
So there are things I cannot.

CAP SAUNDERS.

Get the pot.

(The boy picks up the coffee pot)

HARRY EGERTON.

How I came here I do not know myself.
Some Power has led me though I know not why.
I half remember that I could not sleep
For voices round me in my father's hall,
And rose and wandered forth, fleeing from something
That seemed to follow me across the waste,
A sighing and a thundering of men.
All day, it seems, I've wandered over the mountains
And all last night. Then from afar I spied
Your fire here and came to learn my way.

SILAS MAURY.

Your way lies that way and our way lies this.

(Patten, Maury, Cap Saunders and the boy go off through the darkness,
right rear)

HARVEY ANDERSON.

You must be hungry, pard.

HARRY EGERTON.

No, thank you, no,
Nothing to eat.

HARVEY ANDERSON.

> 'Tain't much, but what it is
> You're welcome to it.

HARRY EGERTON.

> *(Calling after the men)*

> And you will go away
> And leave this great cause hanging in mid air?

VOICE OF SILAS MAURY.

> Tend to your business and we'll tend to ours.

HARVEY ANDERSON.

> Don't mind them; they're damn fools.

HARRY EGERTON.

> *You* understand
> What I have tried to say unto these men;
> You understand, I know.

HARVEY ANDERSON.

> I think I do.

HARRY EGERTON.

> And something tells me we shall meet again.

HARVEY ANDERSON.

> Who knows? I'm tramping round, to-day one place,
> To-morrow another. I'm a rolling stone.
> I never have been one to keep the trails.
> Just knock about the States and watch the plains
> For something—I don't know—and yet 'twill come,
> And when she comes she'll shake her good and hard.
> I don't know what you're rolling in your mind,
> But, as you say, it's a great land we've got.
> I like to lie and feel her under my back
> And know she tumbles to the double seas
> Up to her hips in mile on mile of wheat.
> Beyond that moon are cities packed with men
> That overflow. The fields are filling up.
> They're climbing up the mountains of the West——

HARRY EGERTON.

> *(Looking after the men)*

> And going on beyond them.

Harvey Anderson.

It's all right.
They'll reach the coast off there or reach the ice,
And then they'll have to turn or jump on off.
And they won't jump off. It's too fine a land.
Men throw away the hoofs but not the haunch.
I sometimes see them in the dead of night
Crawling like ants along her big broad back,
With axe and pick and plow, building their hills
And pushing on and on. It's a great land.
And bread tastes good that's eaten in her air.
And there's enough for all here— —

Harry Egerton.

Yes, ah, yes!

Harvey Anderson.

If we could just turn something upside down.
I don't know what you've heard along the waste,
But when you think it's time to ring a change,
And when you draft your men and call the roll,
Write Harvey Anderson up near the top.
And here's my hand, pard. You can count on me.

Harry Egerton.

We'll meet again.

Harvey Anderson.

Hope so. I like your face,
And like the way you talk. Good-night.

Harry Egerton.

Good-night.

*(Harvey Anderson takes up his pack and cast and goes off through the
darkness after the other men. For a long time Harry Egerton stands
looking after him. The fire has burned low)*

Harry Egerton.

Not that, not that! And yet I know 'twill come.
My God! my God! Is there no way, no way?

(Walks left and looks off up the valley)

My father! O my father!

*(He breaks out crying and, staggering about, falls first upon his knees,
then face forward upon the ground. Instantly it becomes pitch dark)*

THE DREAM VISION

*(During the following, a shaft of light, falling upon Harry Egerton,
shows him lying near the boulder. As he cries out, he partially rises, his
form and face convulsed with anguish)*

First Voice.

(From up the mountain, full of pleasure)

Harry! Harry! Come to the heights!

Second Voice.

(From the valley, full of sorrow)

Harry! Harry! Come to the valley!

Third Voice.

(From far back, full of peace)

Harry! Harry! plunge into the darkness,
The abysses and the waterfalls and silence!

The Three Voices.

(In chorus)

We are Realities! We are Realities!

Voice.

(From above)

One life to live!

First Voice.

Come to me, Harry!

Second and Third Voices.

She will grow old.

Voice.

(From above)

One life to live!

Second Voice.

Come to me, Harry!

First and Third Voices.

You cannot help them; you've no power.

Voice.

(From above)

One life to live!

THIRD VOICE.

Come to me, Harry!

FIRST VOICE.

(Gayly)

Fool! fool!

SECOND VOICE.

You cannot die; there is no death.

VOICE.

(From above)

Decide!

HARRY EGERTON.

My God!

VOICE.

(From above)

Decide!

HARRY EGERTON.

My God!

VOICE.

(As of a drunkard singing)

If you was in the gutter, Bill,
And I was on the roof— —

VOICES.

You're going mad! You're going mad!

HARRY EGERTON.

Mother! mother!

(Presently, about twenty feet up in the rear and on either side, faint
lights begin to appear and faint sounds of music are heard. Gradually
the lights brighten a little and the sounds of music become more and
more audible until one becomes conscious that on the left an orchestra
is playing and to the right a piano. One also becomes conscious of a vast
and beautiful hall over the floor of which, as the music plays, the forms

of dancers are gliding. Occasionally from here and there flashes a sparkle as of diamonds, and low rippling laughter is heard. In the foreground for a space of twelve or fifteen feet, cut off from the main hall by the faintest outlines of an immense arch, small groups of elderly people stand about watching the dancers, or saunter right and left into the adjoining apartments. In these apartments also people are seen moving about, and there is a hum of voices as of men and women in conversation. At no time does it become very light, and all that passes seems to pass in a dim shadow world.

It is sufficiently light, however, to enable one to discern the grotesque richness of the hall which, as one sees at a glance, is an elaborate representation of a pine forest, the boles of the trees standing out in beautiful irregularity along the walls, the boughs above in the semi-darkness seeming to disappear in some sort of cathedral roof. There, all about, singly and in clusters, innumerable small globes as though the cones were illuminated. Between the trees, also in relief and life-sized, figures of men at work getting out timber. Forward right, teams dragging logs, and, on the opposite wall, a distant view of a river with rafts floating down. Standing on stumps, huge figures support the arched doorways, of which there is one in the rear wall right, and one centre in each of the side walls. Left rear, the grand staircase with the glow of some hidden lamp shining upon the landing. Here the carved scene upon the wall is that of an inclined trestle-work, with logs going up apparently into some mill above. Below, crouched upon the newel-post and the lower rail, the carved figure of a large mountain lion with a frosted light in its open mouth. Forward from the arched doorway, left, there is no wall from about four feet up, and through this open space, faintly illumined by small hidden lamps, a greenness as of palms and flowers.

The music ceases and the couples break up. Later, the piano begins again, and just inside the main hall Gladys Egerton, in low décolleté and holding her skirts above her ankles, appears dancing ravishingly to the music of the piano)

FIRST LADY.

Isn't she charming!

SECOND LADY.

And that's George that's playing.

(*Holding her skirts high the girl executes a graceful high kick and there is a clapping of hands*)

MEN'S VOICES.

Bravo! bravo! Once more like that, my kitten!

THIRD LADY.

Dear, you may have my Chester!

       (*Laughter*)

FOURTH LADY.

You dance superbly.

GLADYS EGERTON.

I'll take your husband.

       (*Continues dancing*)

MRS. EGERTON.

Why, Gladys Egerton!

A MAN'S VOICE.

Just any time you want him, Gladys.

GLADYS EGERTON.

All right.

A MAN.

       (*Appearing forward right*)

Ladies, the Governor is telling stories.
Out of politeness let's give him a crowd.

  (*Some of the ladies start right, others begin to move about*)

FIFTH LADY.

She'd make a good catch.

SIXTH LADY.

Either she or George would.

THIRD LADY.

       (*Calling aloud*)

Here is another! Now there are thirteen of us.

       (*Laughter*)

FOURTH LADY.

There you're on my toes. Marjorie's after George.

SIXTH LADY.

Your Marge, my dear— —

    (*Glances in the direction of Mrs. Egerton, then whispers*)

Your Marge may have the other.

Fourth Lady.

> Thank you, dear Mrs. Casper, we'll have—gander.
>
> > (*Laughter. They go out right*)

Seventh Lady.

> To have a son like that!

Eighth Lady.

> Yes, what a pity.

Ninth Lady.

> He hasn't anything like the grace of George.

Seventh Lady.

> Nor the accomplishments.

Eighth Lady.

> Nor the education.

Seventh Lady.

> He belongs down in the mill among the men.

Eighth Lady.

> One would have thought, though, at the first reception—
> If only for his mother's sake.

Seventh Lady.

> That's true.

Ninth Lady.

> How old she looks to-night.

Gladys Egerton.

> *(Who has been skipping to the music, whirls in from the main hall)*
> Mother is old.

Ninth Lady.

> I did not mean for you to overhear that.

Gladys Egerton.

> O that's all right. We always do that way.
>
> > *(Continues dancing)*
>
> If you had on your heart what mother has
> You'd look old, too.

EIGHTH LADY.

What did she mean by that?

GLADYS EGERTON.

Leave us alone here just a little while.

(The women go out right)

GLADYS EGERTON.

Mother!

MRS. EGERTON.

Yes, darling.

GLADYS EGERTON.

Mother, where is Harry?

(Dances)

MRS. EGERTON.

I do not know.

GLADYS EGERTON.

It's very embarrassing.
People are whispering. Mother, has no word come?

MRS. EGERTON.

Have you asked your father?

GLADYS EGERTON.

Yes.

(Dances)

Mother, I'm sure
Something has happened to him.

MRS. EGERTON.

Don't, my child,
Don't say that.

GLADYS EGERTON.

(Mysteriously)

Why?

MRS. EGERTON.

Go, child; people are watching us.

GLADYS EGERTON.

I know why! *I* know why!

(*Dances*)

Let go! let go!

MRS. EGERTON.

And please tell Donald that I'm waiting for him.

GLADYS EGERTON.

You're going after flowers, mother; *I* know.

MRS. EGERTON.

Flowers, my child? What for?

GLADYS EGERTON.

For Harry's grave.

MRS. EGERTON.

Why Gladys, Gladys Egerton!

GLADYS EGERTON.

(*Whirling back into the main hall*)

I know.

(*She disappears into the conservatory, left. Alone, Mrs. Egerton stands a pathetic figure. She walks back into the deserted hall and stops and listens as though to the upper part of the walls. She then turns slowly and comes forward again. George Egerton enters quickly from the conservatory*)

GEORGE EGERTON.

Mother!

MRS. EGERTON.

Yes, George.

GEORGE EGERTON.

This is disgraceful, mother.

MRS. EGERTON.

I cannot help it, George.

GEORGE EGERTON.

Where did he go?

Mrs. Egerton.

I've told you, George. Now please don't bother me.

George Egerton.

People are whispering.

Mrs. Egerton.

But what can I do?

George Egerton.

Call to them that he's up in bed with fever,
Or say that he was brought home from the river drowned.

Mrs. Egerton.

(Calling aloud)

It's none of your business, people! Harry's my son.

(She comes forward)

George Egerton.

That wasn't what I said. You are just like him.

*(He turns back and re-enters the conservatory. Mrs. Egerton passes
into the room forward right. The lights in the hall become dimmer)*

Voices.

(From the walls)

Sam! Sam! Sam!

*(There is a silence, then a sigh as of innumerable voices, then a silence
and another sigh and still another)*

Harry Egerton.

My father! O my father!

*(From the conservatory comes a sound of laughter, and a beautiful girl
runs in. A moment later the bloom of a large white chrysanthemum is
thrown in after her. A young man enters. Other couples come in. George
Egerton, evidently master of ceremonies, moves about here and there. A
tuning of instruments is heard. People come from the side rooms. When
all is in readiness, while the dancers, who have taken their positions,
stand waiting for the music to begin, the sighing is again heard)*

George Egerton.

(Exasperated by the delay)

What's the matter there, Melazzini?

(Excusing himself to his partner, he goes toward the conservatory, where the orchestra is stationed. As the sigh is repeated the couples gather together. At the third sigh they scatter, some of them running out through the middle door right, others hurrying forward, one or two of the girls laughing hysterically)

GEORGE EGERTON.

It's just the wind that's blowing through somewhere.

(The people disappear into the apartment right. Charles, the butler, and two maids, badly frightened, come in rear)

GEORGE EGERTON.

Close that door, Charles.

CHARLES.

There's no door open, sir.

(The four come forward, the butler and maids briskly, George Egerton more slowly and with a sort of defiance. They, too, pass out right)

VOICES.

(From the walls)

Sam! Sam! Sam!

(The sighs are repeated)

HARRY EGERTON.

My father! O my father!

(The mountain lion upon the newel-post spits the light from his mouth and it breaks upon the floor. The monster then gets down)

LION.

Chris!

A VOICE.

Yes.

LION.

Mike!

A VOICE.

Here.

LION.

Wes Dicey!

A Voice.

Sure.

Harry Egerton.

(*As though a roll were being called*)

Harvey Anderson!

Lion.

Whose voice was that?

A Voice.

Who's Harvey Anderson?

Second Voice.

There's some spy here.

Lion.

Come down, comrades!

Voices.

(*Above*)

We're fast! we're fast!
Nails in our hands and feet!

Third Voice.

Who's that?

Voices.

(*Below*)

They've danced upon my face! And mine!
And mine! And mine! And mine! And mine!

A Voice.

I've been a door-jamb years and years!

Voices.

(*From round the walls*)

We've held these arches up for ages!

Voices.

(*From far below*)

We're the foundations! Help us, comrades!
Down on the rock here—deeper! deeper!

Voices.

Help us, Sam Williams! Help us, Sam Williams!

Lion.

Come down, comrades!

Voices.

(From far away)

We're the windows!
They made us sand, then made us shine!
We've touched their faces and their hair!

Voices.

(From up the stairs)

We're coming, and there's thousands of us!

Voices.

(Far up)

We're holding up the roof!

Lion.

Come down!
You've held her up too long already!

(There has been a pounding of hammers and a creaking as of timbers being loosened. Sighs and groans fill the hall. The lights burn unsteadily, flashing or going out or glowing with a tint of blue)

Voices.

Help us, Sam Williams! Help us! Help us!

Other Voices.

Let 'em alone! They're scabs! They're scabs!

(Carven figures, still rigid, come from the walls. From everywhere they come, in the most fantastic postures, some hopping with one leg lifted, some gliding with raised axes, others bent and in pairs carrying cross-cut saws, still others with peavies in their hands. Up through the floor all round come dark figures with torches in their caps. Stealthily and with muffled voices they gather about the Lion. Suddenly the pounding ceases and all is still)

A Voice.

He's coming, and the Powers are with him!

Second Voice.

Justice is all we want!

SEVERAL VOICES.

Right! Right!

LION.

Are we one, comrades?

ALL.

We're one! We're one!

A VOICE.

Ask him to release us, Sam!

(*Donald Egerton, with Governor Braddock and Bishop Hardbrooke at his heels, comes hurriedly through the centre door right*)

DONALD EGERTON.

(*Peering about, sees the Figures*)

What does this mean? Back to the walls!

LION.

We are the walls!

FIGURES.

We are the walls!

DONALD EGERTON.

I made you what you are!

LION.

That's true!
And we made you!

FIGURES.

And we made you!

LION.

We made each other!
You are our father and we your mother!

FIGURES.

That's true! That's true!

LION.

And now make us as we made you!

GOVERNOR BRADDOCK.

> Be careful, Colonel Egerton.
> See that one there with axe uplifted!

DONALD EGERTON.

> Braddock, as a citizen of this commonwealth
> I call upon you to enforce the laws!

GOVERNOR BRADDOCK.

> My friends and fellow citizens.
> This is unwise, this course you are pursuing,
> And cannot in the end but injure you.
> The laws were made for these disputes,
> And you like others must obey.

LION.

> He made the laws!

FIGURES.

> He made the laws!

DONALD EGERTON.

> Hear that, Braddock! This is anarchy!

GOVERNOR BRADDOCK.

> I urge you to go peaceably to your homes!

LION.

> Our homes?

FIGURES.

> What homes?

LION.

> We have no homes!

> > *(Egerton says something to the Governor)*

GOVERNOR BRADDOCK.

> Then by the— —

BISHOP HARDBROOKE.

> One moment, brother Egerton;
> One moment, Governor; let me say a word.

> > *(Steps toward the Figures)*

> My brothers,
> If hunger hath driven you here, then know I speak
> For one whose self was hungry, Jesus Christ;
> Yet was he meek and lamb-like. Why do you not
> Go to those places that have been prepared
> By charitable, Christian men and women
> For this very purpose, to relieve distress?
> If you are worthy you will there be fed.

FIGURES.

> Whited sepulchre! He's a whited sepulchre!

> *(They advance toward him)*

BISHOP HARDBROOKE.

> How dare you, armed with Labor's sacred tools
> Which our Lord's father sanctified when he
> Wrought at his wood in Nazareth, how dare you,
> With envy in your hearts, on murder bent,
> Intrude upon the quiet social hour
> Of honorable, law-abiding men?
> God sees you with your axes lifted there.
> And though you fear not law nor anything
> Of man, fear God, for he hath power
> And he can reach you in the uttermost
> Parts of the earth or air, as David saith.

FIGURES.

> The rich man's friend! The rich man's friend!

GOVERNOR BRADDOCK.

> Then by the power vested in me— —

FIGURES.

> We are the power! We are the power!

GOVERNOR BRADDOCK.

> As Governor of this commonwealth
> I will call out the military!

FIGURES.

> We are the military! We are the military!

GOVERNOR BRADDOCK.

> *(Calls)*

> General Chadbourne!

PEOPLE.

> (*Who have been peering in forward right*)

Chadbourne! Chadbourne!

> (*Egerton and the Bishop follow the Governor out centre right, and the people disappear*)

FIGURES.

> (*Aloud*)

Release, release us from this spell!

LION.

Release yourselves!

FIGURES.

> (*With tremendous surprise*)

We can! We can!

> (*There are shouts and a thunder of tools falling upon the floor*)

SHOUTS.

We're free! We're free!

OTHER SHOUTS.

And seize the throats that nailed us fast!

HARRY EGERTON.

Forget the past! Forget the past!

SHOUTS.

An enemy! He's an enemy!

HARRY EGERTON.

Release your brothers!

SHOUTS.

To hell with the scabs!

> (*They rush through the house, right*)

VOICE OF DONALD EGERTON.

Fire on them!

VOICE OF MRS. EGERTON.

No, no, Donald! Shed no blood!
Think of their children!

Voice of Donald Egerton.

Fire, I say!

Men's Voices.

We are your fathers and your brothers!

A Deep Voice.

Fire!

(*A pause*)

Cries.

Treason! Treason!

The Deep Voice.

Shoot them down!

(*Shots are heard and noises as of a riot*)

Harry Egerton.

My God! My God!

(*The noises die away. In the darkness the walls are heard sighing*)

Harry Egerton.

My father! O my father!

(*A pause*)

Voice.

(*Forward right, in the darkness*)

It's mine!

Second Voice.

It's mine!

First Voice.

Let go that hand!

Second Voice.

I had it first!

First Voice.

Hain't you the rubies?

(*Sounds of quarrelling here and there*)

Third Voice.

(Centre right)

Shut up your mouths! You'll have the police here!

VOICES.

(From the walls)

Brothers, help! We're fast! We're fast!

FOURTH VOICE.

Pick up the rug, Pete! Let's be off!

(Forms of men loaded with the spoil of the mansion are seen hurrying
out left)

VOICES.

(Entering right)

'Tain't fair! 'Tain't fair!

FIFTH VOICE.

(Left)

Make for the river!

SIXTH VOICE.

Sam, this ain't fair!

SAM.

(Entering right)

Hold on there, comrades!

VOICES.

Some's got it all and some ain't none!

SAM.

Put down that stuff!

CRIES.

That's right! That's right!
An equal divvy! An equal divvy!

OTHER CRIES.

No, no, you don't! That's mine! That's ours!

SAM.

Comrades, we're one!

CRIES.

(*Of those who have nothing*)

We're one! We're one!

OTHER CRIES.

(*Of those with their arms full*)

Every man for himself! Every man for himself!

(*Sounds of scuffling and fighting*)

CRIES.

Let loose, God damn you! Knock him down!

(*The sounds die away left*)

CRIES.

(*Far left*)

'Tain't fair! 'Tain't fair!

(*The walls are heard sighing*)

VOICE.

(*From above*)

Who will go down
Where all is sorrow, woe, and strife,
Where unshaped things are jostling into life?
Who will go down?

HARRY EGERTON.

I will.

VOICE OF MRS. EGERTON.

(*Full of anguish*)

Harry! Harry!

(*There is a thundering and crashing in the darkness*)

HARRY EGERTON.

(*Quickly staggering to his knees, then to his feet*)

Here! here! Mother! mother!

(*Instantly the darkness disappears. Morning is breaking over the
mountains*)

HARRY EGERTON.

(*Looks about. Clasps his head in his hands*)

Horrible! horrible!

(Sees the ashes of the fire. Recalls the incidents of the early night)

And went away.

(Notices that the boulder is gone. Looks down the slope, left)

The boulder thundering down the steep.
I must have slept upon the ground.
Ah, what is this?

(Gets down on his knees where the boulder lay)

The Mine! *The Mine!* THE MINE!

ACT II
THE MILL

Scene: A street showing, right, the great lumber plant of the Egerton Company. Centre, occupying the greater part of the space between left and right, a sort of common, overstrewn, as such places usually are, with sawdust and waste sawings of the mill, extends back a hundred yards or so to where the river sweeps in from behind a rising slope on the left and disappears behind the high fence of the mill-yard on the right. Across the river, right, the same denuded mountains as were seen in the preceding Act, and, centre, the alluvial stretches of the valley widening out into the plains. Left rear, on this side of the river, a sort of hill comes in and upon its rather steep slope are rows of roughly built plank houses which have evidently been standing many years. They are all of one design and rest in the rear upon the ground, the front being propped up on posts, in some cases six or eight feet high. Of two or three of these shacks it would seem that the occupants had tried to have a garden, for here and there are small green patches as of late turnips, also tall stakes with withered bean vines clinging to them. From the numerous footpaths that come down toward the mill-gate it is evident that these shacks are the homes of the employees of the Egerton Company. The mill-yard on the right is surrounded by a high board-fence. New planks have recently been put in here and there, and on top of the fence, apparently just strung, are several rows of bright new barbed wire. Over the top of the fence and through the open gates of the driveway which is in the corner, a portion of the latter having been cut off for this purpose, are seen countless lumber stacks, and beyond these, far back and facing left, a section of an enormous mill. Along the comb of the roof, doubtless running its full length, is a large red sign with white letters of which one sees only: RTON AND CO.

Before the entrance to the mill-yard two of the State militia with rifles upon their shoulders patrol the property, one of them pacing right and left along the street in the foreground, the other backwards and forwards in the open space that goes toward the river. About twenty feet from the entrance stands a large red automobile, under which, stretched upon his back, lies the chauffeur, with his hands up fixing something.

As the Scene opens, the two sentries, one of them rolling a cigarette, the other with his gun behind his head and with his arms hanging over it, stand listening back toward the mill, where a number of voices are singing, 'There'll Be a Hot Time in the Old Town Tonight.' When the song is finished a cheer goes up.

Time: The afternoon of the next day about four o'clock.

FIRST SENTRY.

All I say is, keep your tobacco dry
And don't go wiring the folks at home
To have your supper warm to-morrow night.

CHAUFFEUR.

They'll be to work, all right, you take my word.

FIRST SENTRY.

There's such a thing as eating words until
Your belly cries for something solider.

CHAUFFEUR.

(Pointing toward the mill)

You see that smoke back there.

FIRST SENTRY.

That's all right, too.
A kid can start a fire.

CHAUFFEUR.

Wait and see.

A MILITIAMAN.

(Who, half way back toward the mill, has climbed upon a lumber stack)

I nominate J. D. for Governor.

A VOICE.

(Farther back, commandingly)

Shut up your mouth up there!

SECOND VOICE.

Will you be good?

(The militiaman gets down from the stack)

SECOND SENTRY.

How large a force is it they're counting on?

CHAUFFEUR.

It's not the force. It's the effect 'twill have.
You let a dog run for another's bone,
You'll see the last dog do some running too.

FIRST SENTRY.

And do some fighting, maybe.

CHAUFFEUR.

> That's up to you.
> The law protects men in their right to work.
>
> > (*The sentries whisper together*)

CHAUFFEUR.

> The old man knows his business. All he says
> Is simply this, 'I'm bringing in the men.
> It's up to you to get them to the mill.'
> You see you don't know everything, my boy.

FIRST SENTRY.

> You work for Egerton, and I don't blame you,
> But when you come right down to solid facts—
> And if you'll clear your eye a bit you'll see it—
> He's got his match in this man Williams.

CHAUFFEUR.

> What!

SECOND SENTRY.

> He's got his match in this man Williams.

CHAUFFEUR.

> C-h-rist!

FIRST SENTRY.

> Figure it out yourself.
>
> > (*He sees Wes Dicey who, with Jim King and Rome Masters, has just
> > come in, right*)
>
> What do you want?

DICEY.

> He knows me.

CHAUFFEUR.

> He's all right.
>
> > (*Careful to keep out of sight of the shacks on the slope, Dicey and his
> > companions whisper together near the fence. The Second Sentry, as
> > though he had been neglecting his duty, goes out right, patrolling his
> > beat*)

FIRST SENTRY.

> It's easy enough

To figure it out, I say. There's thirteen men
Returned to work in five weeks. In an hour
You calculate four hundred will return.
You fellows couldn't count nine pins for me.

(*Dicey and his companions pull their hats down over their eyes, their collars up about their necks, and make briskly for the gate*)

FIRST SENTRY.

(*Starts back on his beat*)

Talk of a man like that running the State.
He'd better learn to run his business first.

(*George Egerton, looking spick and span, comes out of the mill-yard, putting on one of his gloves. He glances at Dicey and his companions as they pass in. Suddenly he turns and whistles after them and saunters back into the mill-yard as if to speak with them*)

GEORGE EGERTON.

(*Coming out a little later*)

O Jack, will you tell mother— —

CHAUFFEUR.

Yes, sir.

GEORGE EGERTON.

(*Provoked*)

What?
Why do you put it that way? Now I've forgot.

(*Continues putting on his glove*)

Tell mother I've inquired of the men
And they've seen nothing of him.

CHAUFFEUR.

Yes, sir.

GEORGE EGERTON.

What?

CHAUFFEUR.

Nothing of Harry, sir.

GEORGE EGERTON.

(*Walks left, then comes back*)

Jack.

CHAUFFEUR.

Yes, sir.

GEORGE EGERTON.

Jack.

(*Looks over in the car*)

Did you find any hair-pins in the car
This morning?

CHAUFFEUR.

Not this morning.

GEORGE EGERTON.

(*Takes a coin from his pocket and hands it to the chauffeur*)

You'll take care.

(*He goes out left, examining his face in a small mirror which he has
taken out with the coin. The Second Sentry has come in right and
stands reading a notice which is tacked on the fence*)

CHAUFFEUR.

By sun-down, don't it?

SECOND SENTRY.

Something of the sort.

CHAUFFEUR.

And the wind sharpening up across the plains.
They'll think twice, won't they, before they stay out?

SECOND SENTRY.

Who signed this name here?

CHAUFFEUR.

Eg—the boss himself.

SECOND SENTRY.

Hell of a hand he writes.

CHAUFFEUR.

Your partner there
Knows about as much of the situation here
As a sea-turtle knows of sassafras.
Talks of a match. There's been no match at all.
The old man's never tried to start the mill.

But let a thing like that go up some day.

(*Buck Bentley with an empty nail keg in his hand comes from the mill-yard and sits down with his back to the farther gate-post and begins to fill his pipe*)

CHAUFFEUR.

If you've heard thunder, one of those loud claps
That ends the winter, and if you'd lived here
And knew the old man's power, then you'd know
I'm shooting low when I say they'll be here,
If they don't all fall dead upon the way.
They've got to make hay now. Days don't stand still
When the old man is moving to and fro.

(*Goes about oiling the machine*)

FIRST SENTRY.

(*Coming forward*)

If Williams comes, I'll tell you what he'll do.
With the big force he'll have behind his back,
He'll lock these gates and coop the old man up
With Jergens and the Chief and all the rest.
Then say, 'Now take me home.' You know the way.
You'll take him to the big house on the hill.

(*The Chauffeur turns and looks at him half in anger, half in contempt*)

FIRST SENTRY.

You won't dare look at him that way.

SECOND SENTRY.

Dan's right.
You fellows, you that shove those things about,
You have a way of knowing who's the lord.

FIRST SENTRY.

Exactly. And this man Williams up and down
Is big as Egerton. And the old man's 'spike'
Will touch him where the tailors say it should.
And if it's lined with silk Williams won't care.
He'll steer the big blow-out this afternoon
And they won't know the difference. It's the front
And the big planet here that people see;
And Williams is as broad as Egerton.

(*A militiaman comes hurrying from the mill-yard*)

MILITIAMAN.

Who's got a cigarette to trade for news?
You couldn't guess it in a thousand years.

SECOND SENTRY.

We're going home.

MILITIAMAN.

Guess high; guess something great.

FIRST SENTRY.

The boys have met the strikers at the station
And we're all going into action.

MILITIAMAN.

Nope.
Something the old man's done.

SECOND SENTRY.

What?

MILITIAMAN.

Put her there.

(The Sentry gives him a cigarette)

Ordered us down a big red tub of punch,
With six or eight kegs of the foaming stuff.

(The Sentries stare comically at one another)

MILITIAMAN.

Well, my tin soldiers? Under a shot like that
To stand as cold as you do!

(Shouts in the ear of the First Sentry)

Punch, old man!

(To himself)

The wind of liquor and they've gone dead drunk!

FIRST SENTRY.

(Starts for the mill-gate, then turns)

Who said 'shut up' when some man back there cried
'Hurrah for Egerton'?

MILITIAMAN.

Cap. Haskell.

FIRST SENTRY.

> (*To the Second Sentry*)

Eh?

SECOND SENTRY.

Haskell to hell.

FIRST SENTRY.

> (*Shouting toward the mill*)

Hurrah for Egerton
For Governor!

SECOND SENTRY.

Hip hurrah!

FIRST SENTRY.

Up with you, Buck!
We'll have no traitors in the camp, by God.
Up on your pins and shout 'Hurrah!' three times.

> (*He seizes Bentley and they wrestle into the mill-yard*)

SECOND SENTRY.

Eight kegs, you say?

MILITIAMAN.

> (*Slapping him on the back*)

And punch, old man, and punch!
Reception punch!

> (*He hurries out toward the mill. Bentley enters, followed by the First Sentry*)

SECOND SENTRY.

What do you think of that?

FIRST SENTRY.

> (*To the Chauffeur, with affected disdain*)

Talk about Williams downing such a man!

FIRST SENTRY.

> (*Nodding toward the Chauffeur*)

And he, too, in the employ of Egerton!

CHAUFFEUR.

Fine pair of knaves! You'll drink his wine all right.

SECOND SENTRY.

(*On his way out, points to the notice*)

Look what a damn fine hand the old man writes.

(*Goes out right*)

FIRST SENTRY.

(*On his way back, to the Chauffeur*)

It's a good thing that some men never tell.

(*Walks slowly, rifle up; then from rear*)

Hurrah for Egerton for Governor!

VOICE OF SECOND SENTRY.

(*Out right*)

Halt!

(*A pause*)

Halt!

(*Buck Bentley rises from the keg and comes forward*)

DO YOU HEAR!

(*The Chauffeur leaps from the car and hurries forward. There is a shot*)

FIRST SENTRY.

(*Running forward*)

Who is it?

MILITIAMAN.

(*Hurrying from the mill-yard*)

What was that?

(*Voices are heard right. A moment later the Second Sentry enters with
Harvey Anderson, who carries in his arms fragments of the cast that
has been broken by the shot*)

SECOND SENTRY.

Where in the hell have you been living
That you don't know enough to stop when— —

HARVEY ANDERSON.

Pard,

If I'd stop every time some man said stop,
I'd still be standing somewhere.

(*He walks left, away from the others, who exchange glances as if amazed at the man's audacity. He lays the largest of the pieces upon the ground, then looks among the others in his arms. Donald Egerton and General Chadbourne, both evidently dressed for a function, the latter being in full military uniform, brand new, come quickly from the mill-yard, followed by Jergens and the Chief of Police*)

CHADBOURNE.

What's the trouble?

SECOND SENTRY.

This man came through the line. I called three times.

CHADBOURNE.

(*To Harvey Anderson*)

Don't you know better than do such a thing?

CAPTAIN HASKELL.

(*Comes from the mill-yard, then turns and calls back*)

Stay where you are. We'll attend to this affair.

EGERTON.

What business have you here?

HARVEY ANDERSON.

I just came down
To look about a bit.

JERGENS.

To look about!
You think we're running a menagerie?
Didn't you see these soldiers? What do you mean?

HARVEY ANDERSON.

(*To the Chief of Police*)

Just step back, pard. I'm neither dog nor bear.

(*Back in the mill-yard militiamen are seen climbing on top of lumber piles to see what the trouble is*)

EGERTON.

Came down from where?

Harvey Anderson.

From up there on the mountains.

Jergens.

To look about for what?

Harvey Anderson.

Just anything—
Just anything that's 'round to see.

(He gets down and begins to fit the pieces together. The men watch him. Suddenly he stops and looks about him)

Did I——

(He rises and goes right to where a piece of the cast lies upon the ground)

Chief of Police.

Shall I take charge of him, Mr. Egerton?
I'll lock him up if you say so.

Chadbourne.

(As Anderson returns)

Don't you know
That when a sentry challenges a man
He's got the right to shoot him in his tracks?

Harvey Anderson.

The risk's on me, pard.

Chadbourne.

Eh!

Harvey Anderson.

The risk's on me.

Chadbourne.

You take care, sir, how you're addressing me.

(Jergens walks rear, takes from his pocket some field glasses, which he polishes with a handkerchief. The Chauffeur joins him. Chadbourne turns and says something vicious to the Second Sentry)

Egerton.

How came you by this thing?

Harvey Anderson.

I'm of the men
That Egerton sent out.

EGERTON.

Jergens, is he
One of our men?

HARVEY ANDERSON.

(*Glancing up*)

You Egerton?

CHIEF OF POLICE.

He is.

JERGENS.

There's many of them that I never saw;
But he's got that, so I suppose he is.

(*He searches the mountains with his glasses. The rest contemplate him
in silence. In Anderson's eyes, as he watches them, there is a strange,
glad light. Indeed throughout the Scene his manner is that of a man
who is hiding a tremendous triumph*)

HASKELL.

He's out here with his glasses every day.

CHADBOURNE.

One of the richest mines in all the West — —

EGERTON.

Very rich mine.

CHADBOURNE.

So I have been informed.

CHIEF OF POLICE.

Been lost for fifty years.

CHADBOURNE.

But with this thing — —

(*Indicating the cast*)

You're almost sure to find it.

SECOND SENTRY.

(*To First Sentry, evidently meaning Chadbourne*)

A damn fool.

EGERTON.

Yes, we expect the signal any day.

(*Dicey, King, and Masters appear just inside the mill-yard and, catching the eye of the Chauffeur, point to Jergens, who, later, hands the glasses to the Chauffeur and goes to Dicey in the mill-yard*)

CHIEF OF POLICE.

The citizens had arranged a demonstration.
Flags were to go up that day and cannon boom,
And Colonel Egerton was to make a speech.

EGERTON.

Yes, Clayton, and I'll tell them something, too.

CHIEF OF POLICE.

I guess they'll be ashamed to have it now.

EGERTON.

Why didn't you stay out on the mountains?

HARVEY ANDERSON.

Well— —

EGERTON.

Get tired?

JERGENS.

Chief!

HARVEY ANDERSON.

Can't say— —

EGERTON.

Then what's the trouble?

(*The Chief of Police joins Jergens and with the three men they disappear in the mill-yard*)

HARVEY ANDERSON.

Well, you see, Mr. Egerton, it's this way:
A man can piece together things like this,
But somehow you can't get hold of that in here
That goes to pieces when your faith breaks up.

EGERTON.

What do you mean?

HARVEY ANDERSON.

I never could find gold;
It don't run in our family.

EGERTON.

Rather late
In your discovery, it seems to me.
Why didn't you think of it when you first went out?

HARVEY ANDERSON.

Well, you know how it is. You've seen a stone
Hang on a mountain side for years sometimes;
You don't know why; you just don't notice it
Until some morning—jump! she thunders down
And wakes a whole town up; then you remember.

(He comes forward and looks off in the direction from which he came as though he were expecting someone)

EGERTON.

(To Chadbourne)

A sort of luck, you see, this getting on.

CHADBOURNE.

Predestination.

EGERTON.

Yes; if a man's rich
He couldn't help but be. There's some old lamp,
An heirloom in his family, that he rubs.
And if he's poor, 'Hard luck.'

CHADBOURNE.

Or been 'ground down.'

EGERTON.

They're told so.

CHADBOURNE.

Egerton's heel.

EGERTON.

Old Egerton's.

> *(They walk toward the automobile)*

CHADBOURNE.

I don't know what the country's coming to.

EGERTON.

Merchants are merchants, Chadbourne.

CHADBOURNE.

I suppose.
Captain, will you get my overcoat?

*(Haskell, who with the Chauffeur has been looking through the glasses,
goes into the mill-yard. A number of militiamen who have been hanging around the gate gather about Anderson and they are soon having a
good time together)*

EGERTON.

What do they care for Country or for Art,
Or any of the higher things of life?
'Give us this day our daily trade.' We live,
We manufacturers, to fill their tills.

CHADBOURNE.

They're sowing dragons' teeth and they don't know it.

EGERTON.

You'll see them to-morrow when I start the mill;
They'll tip their hats when I pass through the streets.
And you could comb the town: they never heard of
Any petition to the Governor,
Nor any contributions, not a one.
They're all staunch friends of mine, and always have been.
'Why, Colonel Egerton, he built this town,
Our leading citizen.' I'll get them though.

CHADBOURNE.

If you could shut down for a season, say.

EGERTON.

That's just what I've been wanting to do, Chadbourne.
Unfortunately, just now we're in a place
Where we can't do as we would like to do;
Or rather Jergens is.

CHADBOURNE.

He told me.

EGERTON.

Yes,
He's got to meet his margins.

CHADBOURNE.

It's too bad.

(*The militiamen laugh out at some story Anderson is telling them*)

EGERTON.

So I can't strike them without striking him.

CHADBOURNE.

I hope you'll find the mine.

A MILITIAMAN.

(*Appearing at the gate*)

'Phone, General.

EGERTON.

I'll show them though that J. D. don't forget.

CHADBOURNE.

Pardon me.

(*He starts for the mill-yard. With a wave of his hand he orders the militiamen back through the gate*)

HARVEY ANDERSON.

(*Aloud, as they draw away*)

And we charging up that Hill
As if we didn't know what canned beef was,
We, when we'd had slow elk[1] out on the plains.

(*Egerton goes rear to the Chauffeur and himself adjusts the glasses to his eyes*)

A MILITIAMAN.

(*As they pass through the gate*)

Stay and have one with us.

HARVEY ANDERSON.

---

[1] *Stolen cattle*

After business hours.

EGERTON.

Where did you leave off?

HARVEY ANDERSON.

Where the big rock hangs
On the south slope up yonder.

>　　*(Dicey, King, and Masters come from the mill-yard, followed by Jer-*
>　　　*gens. Dicey is dividing money with his companions)*

DICEY.

Thank you, boss.

JERGENS.

Then call me up.

DICEY.

I will.

HARVEY ANDERSON.

It ain't there now.

>　　*(The three men go out around the corner right. Jergens joins Egerton*
>　　　*and the Chauffeur. Harvey Anderson watches them in silence)*

HARVEY ANDERSON.

And that's another reason I came down
To hear those cannon boom and see those flags.
You'll have a band play too?

*(With his eyes fixed upon them he slowly shoves his foot through the cast
and it falls to pieces. He stands still for a moment. He then picks up his
hatchet and roll of blankets, and, going to the gate, throws them into the
mill-yard. He does the same with the fragments of the cast, first carrying
an armful which he empties inside, then coming back and picking up the
last two or three pieces, which he jerks in after the others.*

*The First Sentry, coming from rear, signals to the Second Sentry, who
is passing on his beat. The latter waits and, having heard what the
former had to say, starts off)*

SECOND SENTRY.

>　　　　　*(Evidently quoting Chadbourne)*

'Tried to get smart
And hit the cast to see the pieces fly.'

(*The First Sentry starts back on his beat, laughing*)

HARVEY ANDERSON.

(*As the Second Sentry passes him*)

It's steel you're shooting, ain't it?

SECOND SENTRY.

Go to hell.

(*Goes out*)

HARVEY ANDERSON.

It's all right, partner.

(*Like a great boy he stands tossing his hat into the air and trying to catch it. Egerton and Jergens regard him and seem to be saying something about him. Jergens goes into the mill-yard*)

EGERTON.

(*Comes to Anderson*)

In the line of work,
What have you ever done?

HARVEY ANDERSON.

Most everything,
From punching cattle down to hunting gold.
But chiefly knocked about among the States.

EGERTON.

Drinking and gambling?

HARVEY ANDERSON.

Some of that in too.

(*The Chauffeur goes into the mill-yard*)

EGERTON.

There's something in you that I like, my man.
You go about things in a way. And then
The daring that you showed. You're full of life;
A man can see that. Tended cattle, eh?
Think you could govern men and round them up
If need be?

HARVEY ANDERSON.

I don't know.

(*Tosses his hat into the air*)

EGERTON.

> You don't belong
> To a Union?

HARVEY ANDERSON.

> No.

EGERTON.

> You're not the sort of man
> To stand dictation. You've a work to do,
> Men of your type. I think I heard you say
> That you were with the rangers at San Juan?

HARVEY ANDERSON.

> I did some time down there.

EGERTON.

> Well spent, my boy.
> I had a brother in the Civil War.

> (*Watches Anderson catching his hat*)

> That was a good one. I know how you feel;
> So full of life you don't care what comes on.
> 'Out of the way!' It's rare enough these days.
> You'd be surprised what cowards most men are,
> Big six foot fellows who want to go to work;
> Offer it to them and they shake their heads
> Because they see some pickets round the corner.

HARVEY ANDERSON.

> 'Fraid of your soldiers?

EGERTON.

> Pickets; Union men.
> They'd fly to arms quick enough if Charlie Hare—
> Charlie's our Mayor—said 'No more free speech.'
> But Williams he can say, 'No more free work.'
> They'd rather talk, you see, than be free men.

HARVEY ANDERSON.

> That's a good phrase, 'Free Work.'

EGERTON.

> A good 'phrase,' yes.

HARVEY ANDERSON.

We ought to put that in our Bill of Rights.

EGERTON.

Our Bill of Rights, my boy, 's no more than air.
It's men to back it up. We've gone to seed
In Sabbath speculations on men's rights.
What we need now is Monday morning's work.

HARVEY ANDERSON.

This Williams, I suppose, has gotten rich
Controlling all these men?

EGERTON.

That I don't know.
It's not so much the few that he controls
As the large numbers they intimidate.

HARVEY ANDERSON.

Got to accept his terms or not work, eh?

EGERTON.

They have a thing they call the 'Union Scale.'

(*Looks at his watch*)

HARVEY ANDERSON.

And these men that can't work, they stand for that,
Having no voice at all in their affairs?

EGERTON.

They don't see; they're a lot of ignorant men.

HARVEY ANDERSON.

Why don't you show them?

(*Egerton smiles, walks to the gate and listens, then comes back*)

EGERTON.

Out on the plains, my boy,
Tending your cattle, did you speak with them
And reason with them?

HARVEY ANDERSON.

With the cattle?

EGERTON.

Yes.

Harvey Anderson.

It all depends upon the mood they're in.
Sometimes a man can just sit on his horse,
If the feed's good; and sometimes in the night,
If a storm's brewing, then it's best to sing;
Go round them this way —

    (*Circles and sings one of the strange melodies of the cowboys*)

for they're restless then.

Egerton.

Sing to your cattle?

Harvey Anderson.

Let them know you're friends
All out together and a big storm on.

Egerton.

That's interesting.

    (*Anderson comes forward and looks off right, the direction from which
    he came, as though he were expecting some one*)

Egerton.

We've got an opening here
I think would suit you.

Harvey Anderson.

Well.

Egerton.

In half an hour,
Or less than that, there'll be a lot of men
Come from the station, the force I'm bringing in,
Guarded by soldiers; then, if I guess right,
The Union—they'll be crowding here for work,
Wanting to go to work, you understand,
But with their eye on Williams. He'll say 'No.'
But there's another faction will say 'Yes.'

Harvey Anderson.

And while they're balanced — —

Egerton.

That's just what I want.
You've got a good cool head, and you know men.
And then you have a way of putting things.

HARVEY ANDERSON.

Make 'em a little speech?

EGERTON.

I don't care how.

HARVEY ANDERSON.

Just get 'em in your pen, eh?

EGERTON.

It's their last chance.
And I can say, my boy, if you make good
And prove to be the man we're looking for,
I'll push you on as fast as you can go.
My partner here was one that proved himself.
And then next year we'll take my other mills
And break this Union thing or we'll know why.
A shot or two for your own land, you see.

HARVEY ANDERSON.

Free Work.

EGERTON.

Free Mills.

HARVEY ANDERSON.

Free men.

(Starts left)

EGERTON.

You know the way?

(Egerton turns and goes into the mill-yard)

SECOND SENTRY.

(Comes in right and meets the First Sentry, who has just come forward)

Damn stuck-up fool! Just because Egerton
Invites him to his house.

FIRST SENTRY.

He's got a corn.

SECOND SENTRY.

> I hope they'll tramp it off.

> (*The First Sentry quickly signals that some one is coming toward the gate*)

SECOND SENTRY.

> God, I don't care.

> (*The Chauffeur comes hurriedly from the mill-yard and goes and gets into the car. A moment later General Chadbourne and Captain Haskell appear*)

CHADBOURNE.

> And I'll be there till nine or ten o'clock,
> Or even later, for we've some important
> Matters to attend to. And besides
> It's going to be a very fine affair.

HASKELL.

> All right, sir.

CHADBOURNE.

> You won't need me, though, I'm sure.
> Things seem to be all quiet at the station.

SECOND SENTRY.

> (*As he goes out*)

> Ass!

HASKELL.

> We'll break camp to-morrow, I suppose

CHADBOURNE.

> *That's* what I had in mind a while ago!
> I'm glad you spoke of it. When they pass these gates,
> You be here, Haskell, and you get me word.
> I want to be the first to break the news
> To Egerton and the Governor; want to say:
> 'I have the honor to report to you,
> Your Excellency,
> And it gives me pleasure to announce to you
> Upon the occasion of the opening
> Of your new mansion, Colonel Egerton,
> This bit of news, sir, from the military,
> And I offer it with our congratulations,

The strike is over — —'

VOICE OF JERGENS.

(*Back in the mill-yard*)

General Chadbourne!

CHADBOURNE.

Yes! —
'The men have yielded and have gone to work;
And all's been done without one drop of bloodshed,
Thanks to the Governor and to your co-operation
And to the splendid service of the boys.
To-morrow we break camp and go our ways.
Health to you and long life and peace hereafter
In your new home.' Or something of the sort.
I haven't whipped it into final shape.

HASKELL.

And got off, I suppose, with glasses lifted.
'Twill be a nice green feather in our cap.

CHADBOURNE.

And duty done, it's well to have big friends.
There's that old question of the armory;
I'm going to try to jam it through this session.
And besides that —

(*Calls toward the gate*)

What's up?

JERGENS.

(*Enters with the Chief of Police*)

How large a force
Did you send to the station?

CHADBOURNE.

Why do you ask?

JERGENS.

There's talk of violence among the men.

CHIEF OF POLICE.

Some even go so far as to advocate
Marching upon — —

JERGENS.

> That, Chief, may all be bluster.
> For this man Dicey—these men have a way
> Of making things look bad to extort money
> And earn them credit if they turn out well.

CHIEF OF POLICE.

> As a precaution though.

JERGENS.

> I've no objection.

> > (*Egerton comes from the mill-yard*)

CHIEF OF POLICE.

> You'd better throw a guard about the house.
> You see it's out of my jurisdiction.

EGERTON.

> Coming to see me, eh?

JERGENS.

> I don't believe it.

> > (*Chadbourne talks aside with Haskell*)

CHIEF OF POLICE.

> To see the Governor, they say.

EGERTON.

> All right.

> > (*Gets into the automobile*)

> They'll find him in the southwest room upstairs
> When the train comes. Have them clean off their feet.

RALPH ARDSLEY.

> > (*Who has just come in, left*)

> Clean off whose feet?

EGERTON.

> Yours, Ardsley. Step right in.

> > (*The Chief of Police goes out, left*)

RALPH ARDSLEY.

> What's the news now?

EGERTON.

> The news is that you've got
> Barely an hour to get on your togs.

> (*Ardsley unbuttons his light overcoat and shows his full dress*)

EGERTON.

> You editors are smart men.

> (*Chadbourne gets in behind with Egerton, Ardsley in front with the
> Chauffeur*)

CHADBOURNE.

> (*As they go out right*)

> Don't forget, Haskell.

*(Jergens lingers about as though undecided what to do. Finally he goes
left and saunters down the street. Haskell enters the mill-yard. Later
an old woman, who has evidently been waiting till the mill-owners left,
comes down the hill-side rear left and begins to pick up sticks that lie
scattered about in the sawdust)*

FIRST SENTRY.

> (*Who finally sees her*)

> Get out!

OLD WOMAN.

> They're thrown away.

BUCK BENTLEY.

> (*Who has come from the mill-yard and resumed his seat on the keg*)

> Let her alone.

OLD WOMAN.

> God help us if we can't have even sticks
> That's thrown out.

FIRST SENTRY.

> Let your old man go to work.

OLD WOMAN.

> Then let 'em pay fair wages. Ain't they all
> Wantin' to work? What's the poor to do,
> Things goin' up an' wages goin' down?
> What's the poor to do?

FIRST SENTRY.

That's your look-out. Move on!

(*He starts toward the old woman. Buck Bentley knocks the ashes from his pipe and goes toward the First Sentry*)

SECOND SENTRY.

(*Who has been watching*)

Know what you're doing, Buck?

(*There is a fight. Bentley takes the rifle from the First Sentry who, in a rage, starts for the gate*)

FIRST SENTRY.

If this goes by
I'll show the regiment a thing or two,
I'll jump the Service, that's what I'll do.

(*He hurries into the mill-yard. Bentley helps the old woman pick up the sticks*)

OLD WOMAN.

I thought they'd never go. God bless you, son.

(*Starts up the slope*)

SECOND SENTRY.

We'll see, by God, who's running this shebang.

OLD WOMAN.

You ain't heard nothin' from the station yet?

BUCK BENTLEY.

No, mother.

(*The old woman goes out. Bentley comes to the gate and sets the rifle against the fence*)

SECOND SENTRY.

(*Talking into the mill-yard*)

He even helped her fill her apron.

HASKELL.

(*Entering with the First Sentry*)

Have you gone crazy, Buck? What do you mean?

BUCK BENTLEY.

(*Fills his pipe*)

Is this the Company's property out here?

HASKELL.

We've got our orders and that settles it.
Don't settle it with you, eh?

A MILITIAMAN.

(*From the top of a lumber stack*)

Here they come!

FIRST SENTRY.

In other words you'll do as you damn please.

(*Haskell comes forward and looks down the street, left*)

HASKELL.

Now shut your mouths.

FIRST SENTRY.

I'm not through with this yet.

(*Picks up his rifle and goes back on his beat*)

SECOND SENTRY.

Damn pretty soldier you are.

HASKELL.

Do you hear?

(*Militiamen are seen climbing on top of the lumber stacks. Others appear at the gate. Captain Haskell walks left where a noise is heard down the street. Presently a squad of militia enters with fifteen or twenty strike-breakers. Behind them, with the officer in charge, comes Jergens, who is speaking to the crowd of strikers that follows. In front of the crowd walks Sam Williams. Mingling among the men are seen Dicey, King, and Masters. Some women and children straggle in and linger, left. On this side of the crowd, silent, watching everything, is Harvey Anderson*)

JERGENS.

The world is big and we can get the men.

SAM WILLIAMS.

That's all right, Mr. Jergens.

JERGENS.

All we want,

And more too.

Sam Williams.

That's all right.

Jergens.

We've shown you that.
If not, stick it out; that's all I've got to say.

Sam Williams.

The point is now about the saws. Will you
Put the guards on?

Voice.

(From the crowd)

There where the boys were killed.

Jergens.

We will or will not, as it suits ourselves.

Voice.

(From the crowd)

About our places, Sam.

Sam Williams.

If they come back,
You'll give the boys the places that they had,
All of them?

(The militia, with the strike-breakers, pass into the mill-yard)

Voice..

(From the crowd)

Will we get our places back?

Jergens.

The places that have not been filled are yours.
As for discharging men that we've brought here,
Not one.

(He says something to Haskell, then turns to the crowd)

Now just one word. When these gates close,
You're out. You understand that, do you? Out
Not for to-day, to-morrow, or six weeks,
But all time. You've got just ten minutes left.

Then, Captain, close these gates.

HASKELL.

All right, sir.

(Jergens passes into the mill-yard)

VOICE.

(From the crowd)

Well?

ANOTHER VOICE.

What do you say, Sam?

JIM KING.

Williams has had his say.
And you see where we are.

ROME MASTERS.

Hear Wes!

JIM KING.

Wes!

SEVERAL.

Sam!

SAM WILLIAMS.

I don't know, comrades, as I ought to say,
Seeing as I don't gain or lose in this.
For I'm of them that have no place in there.
But if you want my — —

CRIES.

Yes, go on! Go on!

SAM WILLIAMS.

Well, comrades, it's the Union first with me.
That props the rest. You take that prop away
And everything comes down. We've climbed a bit
Since we first organized. And what we've won,
What is it that keeps it won? The Union, comrades,
Is just another name for all of us.

JERGENS.

(Appearing at the gate)

Another thing. If you don't come to work
We'll want those shacks up there. Remember that.

> (*Goes out*)

SAM WILLIAMS.

And we need something bigger than we are,
Don't we, if they do with their mills and lands?
You heard Aug. Jergens what he said just now
When Chris here called to him, 'But you unite.'
You heard him say, 'That's none of your affair.'
Then how's it their affair if we unite?
Logs you can't handle, but you saw them up,
Then you can handle them. It's the same with us;
They want to handle us to suit themselves.
Comrades, I don't see if you go in there
How you'll not have to come out here again;
Unless you mean to bear whatever comes.
You'll hear no big voice, 'Then we'll all go out,'
That's kept their hands from off you many a time.
Or is it their mercy that you're counting on?
Poor hold you've got there. One window yonder
Of Egerton's big house would put the guards
About the saws. But you hear what he says.
And it's our lives he's talking of.

A WOMAN.

> (*To another who begins to cry*)

Never mind.

SAM WILLIAMS.

What is it that gives him power to talk that way?
Why is it he can do that,

> (*Lifts his hand*)

and trains come in
With soldiers? We can't do it. And they're two
And we're four hundred.

JIM KING.

That don't get us bread.

SAM WILLIAMS.

Is it because they own the mills and lands?
It's only when they own us that they're strong.
Comrades, you've come now where the ways divide.

There's bigger gates than these stand open here
If you'll just stick together. 'Tain't to-day
I'm thinking of. There's a green shore somewhere
If you'll just turn your faces from that gate.
But if you're going to give your Union up
When they say if you don't we'll close these gates,
You'll have no peace. They'll hold it over you
To force you down. Comrades, the day will come
When you'll regret it if you go in there,
Giving your Union up. But that's with you.

CHRIS KNUDSON.

Sam's right. We can't be slaves, men.

KING AND MASTERS.

Wes! Hear Wes!

CHRIS KNUDSON.

Let's march on out to Egerton's big house
And call the Governor out and lay our case
Before him.

CRIES.

Right! That's right!

A VOICE.

First let's go home
And get the women folk and all march out.

MIKE HAWLEY.

You talk like fools. Ain't Braddock, too, a slave?
He's 'bout as big to Egerton as your thumb.

WES DICEY.

It seems to me like, boys, we're in a boat.
We've pulled together hard as any men
Tryin' to make the shore off there. But here
She's leakin' and our biscuits have give out.
The question now is, hadn't we better make
For this shore here? It ain't the one we want;
But here there's bread and water. But they say—
And this it is that seems to rub Sam most—
'Scuttle your boat or you don't land here.' Well,
Scuttle her, then I say.

                              (*Hisses from the crowd*)

Now you hold on.
I love the Union much as any man.
And I've stood by her, too, through thick and thin.
Ain't I stood by her, boys?

JIM KING.

Wes is our friend.

WES DICEY.

And will again. Then what do I mean? Just this:
It's a queer shore ain't got a cove or two
Where you can hide her. I don't mean to say
That Sam ain't done his best to captain us;
He has. But here she is, she's goin' down,
So I say land. For bread tastes mighty good,
And air this time o' year won't keep you warm
If you're turned out. Later, we get our strength,
We'll patch her up and make for that green shore
Sam talks of. But just now it's this or this.

> (*Points toward the mill, then to the ground*)

And if we go down, then where's your Union? Eh?

A VOICE.

He's right.

ROME MASTERS.

But if we live, then it lives too.

WES DICEY.

So it's the Union that I'm speakin' for.

JIM KING.

He's speakin' for our wives and children too.

A VOICE.

What about us whose places have been filled?

ANOTHER VOICE.

You want us all to go down, eh?

SAM WILLIAMS.

No!

SEVERAL.

No!

HARVEY ANDERSON.

Pards,
I'm one of Egerton's men, if you'll let me
Butt in here just a minute with a word.
You've seen two sides of this thing, but there's three.
There's one big black one you don't face at all,
Even your Captain here. You're all right, pard,
In what you say about their mills and lands
Not giving them power; it's their owning you.
And if you'll just tear up that bill of sale
And call the deal off, Egerton's big shadow
That fills the valley, lengthening year by year
Until your hair stands up, you'll be surprised
How you can cover it with a six-foot pole.
For it's on you he's standing.

WES DICEY.

Who are you?

HARVEY ANDERSON.

But look here, pards, are you calling off this sale
Or simply trying, as it seems to me,
To make him take the goods at the old price?

HASKELL.

What have you got to do with it?

HARVEY ANDERSON.

And what's the price?
Where's all that gone?

(Points to the mountains)

Were those just weeds up there
That's been cleared off to get a better view?
Or Christmas trees?

JIM KING.

Who are you?

HARVEY ANDERSON.

And loaded, too,
With food and clothes and homes and silks and gems
And punch that bubbles till she runs down here,
Flushing the soldier boys until they're gay
And on their mettle. Is his name Egerton
That planted all those pines?

>   (*Points to the sky*)

WES DICEY.

What's it to you?

HARVEY ANDERSON.

Worked all these years and yet you've got no bread?

HASKELL.

>   (*Coming toward him*)

What business is it of yours what these men do?

HARVEY ANDERSON.

Handled all that and yet you've got no roof
To cover you!

BUCK BENTLEY.

>   (*Following Haskell*)

Look here, Cap.

HARVEY ANDERSON.

And this man comes
And cracks his whip, 'We'll oust you.' What do you say?

BUCK BENTLEY.

We came down here to see the square thing done,
Not to take sides and try to break this strike.

>   (*Haskell stares at him in amazement*)

HARVEY ANDERSON.

What's your name?

BUCK BENTLEY.

Bentley.

HARVEY ANDERSON.

I'll remember that.
And my name's Anderson.

>   (*They shake hands*)

HASKELL.

>   (*Beckoning to the militiamen about the gate*)

Three or four of you.
I give you ten days in the guard house, Buck.

HARVEY ANDERSON.

You won't be there two hours, pard, take my word.
There's something going to drop here pretty soon.

HASKELL.

(Calls after the militiamen)

Tell Mr. Jergens to step here a minute.

(Bentley is led away into the mill-yard)

HARVEY ANDERSON.

(To the crowd)

God playing Santa Claus among the pines—
Why ain't you fellows had your stockings up?
Or if you have, what are you doing here
Weighing yourselves out on the same old scales,
Men against bread? Pard, let me ask you this:
Suppose you do land with your Union boat,
The bosses on the shore saying all right;
What is it you land for? Grub for another cruise?
And you'll go back then to the fishing grounds
And sink your nets again? Who'll get the catch
This time? Them that's had it all these years?
You've made a big haul here, it seems to me,
Minnows and all. Hundreds of miles like that.
When are you fellows going to dry your nets,
Haul up your boat and say, 'Let's weigh the fish'?
What do you say, pard?

SAM WILLIAMS.

You a Union man?

HARVEY ANDERSON.

I don't know much about your Union, pard.
It's all right, I suppose, far as it goes.
But tell me this—and here's your black side, men—
Long as they own the sea

(Points to the mountains and the plains)

and own the shore,

(Points to the mill)

You think they'll care much, pard, who owns the boat?
And how'll they not own you? You tell me that.

(Williams and the crowd stand silent)

Harvey Anderson.

What do you say?

Haskell.

(*Watch in hand*)

You've got two minutes left.

Harvey Anderson.

Two minutes left of freedom. What do you say?
You've got no North to look to, you white men.

A Woman.

(*With a child in her arms*)

If you go in there, John, don't you come home.

Harvey Anderson.

Bully for you, sister!

The Woman.

Don't you dare come home.
We ain't starved with you, you to sell yourself.

Wes Dicey.

It's either go back, boys, or we'll be tramps.

Harvey Anderson.

There's thousands of them off there good as you.
You'd sell your soul to Egerton for bread.
They keep theirs and go round the back door.

Voice.

(*From the crowd*)

Well?

Jim King.

Listen to me.

Sam Williams.

Comrades, they can't start up;
They've not the men.

Wes Dicey.

Suppose they *don't* start up?
Suppose they shut down till the ice blocks there?

Then where'll we be?

JIM KING.

You'll hear the children cry.

HARVEY ANDERSON.

Shut up your mouths or, if you're married men,
Let your wives speak. 'You'll hear the children cry!'
Where in the hell do you hail from any way?
Or have they starved you till you've lost your grit?

HASKELL.

One minute.

VOICE.

(From the crowd)

Bread!

ANOTHER.

What will we do, Sam?

ANOTHER.

Vote!

SAM WILLIAMS.

I've said my last word.

WES DICEY.

We've no time to vote.

VOICE.

(From afar, right)

Wait!

JIM KING.

Be quick.

HARVEY ANDERSON.

Hold on!

WES DICEY.

Boys, suppose they say,
'First come, first served, and we don't need the rest'?

JIM KING.

> *(Calling attention to the first flakes of snow)*

Look at these flakes, men!

> *(There is a stampede for the gate)*

AN OLD WOMAN.

Run, Tommy!

HARVEY ANDERSON.

> *(Drawing from his pocket a long blue revolver)*

Halt!
The first man puts his foot inside that gate
I'll kill him.

VOICE.

> *(Right as before, now near by)*

One word before you go in there!

> *(Harry Egerton enters breathless)*

HARRY EGERTON.

Pardon me; I have run some seven miles
To be here ere the sun went down, for I
Knew what it meant to you.

> *(Stands for a moment collecting himself)*

Men, my friends,
What is it you are about to do?

HARVEY ANDERSON.

They're going back.

HARVEY ANDERSON.

> *(As Harry Egerton seems about to speak)*

Now listen, boys, for now you'll hear a word
That you'll remember till the crack o' doom.

HARRY EGERTON.

I wouldn't do it, friends, if I were you.
What will to-morrow be and the next day
And years to come if you surrender now?
You have your strength and right is on your side.
I in my father's offices have struck
The balances between you men and him.
I know what part you've had of all these trees
And what part he has had, and in my heart

I know there is a balance on your side.
Things can't go on forever in this way.

HARVEY ANDERSON.

Now the snow falls they're afraid the wolf will howl.

HARRY EGERTON.

Will you be stronger then a year from now,
Your Union broken up, your wages less,
And this defeat behind you dampening all?
Or do you intend henceforth never to lift
The voice of protest, silent whatever comes?
God will provide, my friends. Do not give up.

HARVEY ANDERSON.

(Comes to him)

Tell 'em about it, partner.

HARRY EGERTON.

Not yet.

HARVEY ANDERSON.

Why?

HARRY EGERTON.

Their enemies would say it was the gold.
And we must show them that they're wrong.

A WORKMAN.

Look out!

JERGENS.

(With a stick he has picked up comes from the mill-yard)

What do you mean by interfering here?

*(He discovers Harvey Anderson talking with Harry Egerton and turns,
evidently for an explanation, to Haskell)*

HARVEY ANDERSON.

You've filed your claim though?

HARRY EGERTON.

Yes.

*(Jubilant, Harvey Anderson turns and, catching up one of the mill-
boys, lifts him over his head and slides him down his back, holding him*

by the feet. Jergens advances toward him)

A Workman.

Look out, comrade!

Harvey Anderson.

I wouldn't try it, pard, if I were you.

Jergens.

(To the men)

You'll rue this day!

(To Harvey Anderson)

We'll fix you!

(To the militia)

Close these gates!

(Glowers at Harry Egerton)

Clear these streets, Captain!

Harry Egerton.

Stand where you are, my friends.

Jergens.

Captain, I order you to clear these streets.

Harry Egerton.

Be careful, Captain Haskell, what you do.
This is a public place.

A Militiaman.

What's the word, Cap.?

Haskell.

(To the militiaman, irritably)

Who's in command here, I should like to know?

Jergens.

Your father will attend to you, young man.

(Beside himself with rage, disappears down the street, left)

Harry Egerton.

Now then go quietly to your homes, my friends,
And I to-night will see what I can do.

Sam Williams.

> *(Comes toward him)*

Mr. Egerton.

> *(Holds out his hand)*

Harry Egerton.

Yes, Sam.

> *(Takes his hand)*

Sam Williams.

> *(To the crowd)*

Comrades,
I never thought we'd live to see this day.

> *(The men crowd about them)*

Harry Egerton.

Some of you men are hungry.

The Men.

We're all right!
We're all right, Mr. Egerton!

Harry Egerton.

But never mind.
We will begin a new age in this land.

Harvey Anderson.

Up with your hats, pards! God's on the mountains!

(Tosses his hat into the air. The workmen, in an almost religious ecstasy, go out left, crowding around Harry Egerton and Harvey Anderson. Dicey, King and Masters remain behind, whispering together, then follow the crowd. The militiamen, most of them silent with amazement at the scene they have witnessed, gradually disappear into the mill-yard)

First Militiaman.

I'm for young Egerton if it comes to that.

Second Militiaman.

Most of us boys are sons of workingmen.

Third Militiaman.

I never thought of that.

FOURTH MILITIAMAN.

> Buck's about right, too, kids.
> We came here to see the square thing done,
> Not to be half-sole to the old man's boot.

FIRST MILITIAMAN.

> Let's set Buck free.

SECOND MILITIAMAN.

> What do you say, kids?
>
> > (*They go into the mill-yard, talking earnestly*)

SECOND SENTRY.

> Dan!
>
> > (*The First Sentry joins him and they whisper together*)

FIRST SENTRY.

> > (*Starts with the other for the gate*)
>
> I've nothing against Buck.

SECOND SENTRY.

> Haskell's too fast.
>
> > (*They enter the mill-yard*)

ACT III

THE MANSION

Scene: The great reception hall in the Egerton mansion. One sees at a glance that this is the original of the shadow hall shown in the Dream-Vision in the First Act. The carved mountain lion crouches upon the newel-post, and upon the walls the figures of men at work among the pines are identical with those of the Vision. But here, seen under a natural light, the grotesque grandeur of it all stands out in clear relief. Forward, left and right, just where the great arch separating the main hall comes down, groups of little pines in tubs lend a freshness to the scene.

A brilliant company is gathered. Everywhere, from gestures and lifted eyes, it is evident that the mansion, especially the strange scene upon the walls, is the chief topic of talk among the guests. Centre right, about the piano, a number of young people are watching a couple that is out upon the floor, apparently practising a new step. Near the pines, forward left, General Chadbourne turns from the butler, with whom he has been speaking, to shake hands with some ladies. Later, Ralph Ardsley appears just inside the door, forward right, and holds up a glass of wine. Two or three men notice him and nudge their companions, and one after another saunter past Ardsley into the side room.

Time: The same afternoon about five o'clock.

RALPH ARDSLEY.

Get me the eye of Chadbourne.

FIRST MAN.

General!

(*Out on the floor the couple that is waltzing jostles an elderly lady*)

LADY IN BLACK.

Why can't they wait until— —

ELDERLY LADY.

Now run away.
You've got all night for this tomfoolery.

MRS. EGERTON.

George!

(The young people gradually drift out into the conservatory)

CHADBOURNE.

(Rejoining the Butler)

For it's something that concerns the strike.

BUTLER.

Yes, sir.

CHADBOURNE.

And it's important.

BUTLER.

Yes, sir.

SECOND MAN.

General!

CHADBOURNE.

And I'll be right out— —

(Sees the lifted hand)

I'll be right in here.

(Joins the Second Man, and the two, with Ardsley, disappear into the side room)

YOUNG MATRON.

Why do you men keep going out that way?

THIRD MAN.

(With a wink)

The Governor wants to see us.

(They go into the room, forward right)

LADY WITH CONSPICUOUS COIFFURE.

(Entering forward left with Pale Lady)

Indeed it would;
To just have all the money that you want.

PALE LADY.

And her new necklace, did you notice it?

LADY WITH CONSPICUOUS COIFFURE.

Her mother's plain enough.

PALE LADY.

There she goes now.

(*They pass rear and mingle with the throng*)

FIRST MAN.

(*Appearing forward right with a glass of wine*)

You ladies, I presume, are temperance workers.

(*'The punch! The punch!' is whispered about, and the people begin to pass out centre and forward right*)

FAT LADY.

I mean to just taste everything there is.

(*Goes out*)

LADY IN BLACK.

Isn't it just too grand for anything!

PALE LADY.

At night, though, I should think 'twould scare a body
With all those horrid things upon the walls.

(*They go out. A moment later Mrs. Egerton comes in and looks about as though she were seeking some one*)

MRS. EGERTON.

(*To her daughter, who passes toward the conservatory*)

Please don't keep showing it, Gladys.

GLADYS EGERTON.

Marjorie!

(*She enters the conservatory*)

MRS. EGERTON.

(*Beckons to some one in the room forward left. The Butler appears*)

Has no word come?

BUTLER.

Jack says that Mr. George inquired
And they've seen nothing of him.

(*He goes back into the room, forward left. Mrs. Egerton lingers a while, then returns to the room, forward right. Here, a moment later Ralph Ardsley appears*)

RALPH ARDSLEY.

>*(Calls to a group of four men back near the stairs)*

Laggards! laggards!

>*(Bishop Hardbrooke and a fellow-townsman, each with a man who is evidently a stranger, come slowly forward)*

BISHOP HARDBROOKE.

Isn't there aspiration in all this,

>*(Indicating the house)*

A reaching out toward God, and a love, too,
Of all that God hath made?

FELLOW-TOWNSMAN.

The river there.

RALPH ARDSLEY.

The walls will be here when the wine is gone.

FIRST STRANGER.

But public sentiment.

BISHOP HARDBROOKE.

Vox populi.

FELLOW-TOWNSMAN.

People don't stop to think of what he's done.

BISHOP HARDBROOKE.

Exactly. When an axe falls on one's toes,
The service that it's been, that's out of mind.
And yet you throw the bruise, the moment's pain,
In one side, and in the other a cleared land
With homes and fields— —

SECOND STRANGER.

That's true.

BISHOP HARDBROOKE.

And populous towns.
The balance will be struck up yonder, brother.

RALPH ARDSLEY.

Show me one man that's in the public eye
Because he stands for something, towers above them,

That hasn't had them yelping at his heels.

BISHOP HARDBROOKE.

You know the Editor of the Courier?

> (*The Strangers shake hands with Ardsley*)

SECOND STRANGER.

You didn't come back.

RALPH ARDSLEY.

I've troubles of my own.

> (*Walks back in the hall*)

SECOND STRANGER.

We were together in the Legislature.

BISHOP HARDBROOKE.

> (*Stopping near the door, forward right, as if for a final word*)

Speaking of Egerton, some years ago
I saw that statue in the New York harbor,
The sea mists blown about it, now the head
And now an outflash of tremendous bronze
About the waist. 'Is that the thing,' said I,
'They talk so much about?' Next day 'twas clear.

FIRST STRANGER.

Looked very different.

BISHOP HARDBROOKE.

It's the same with men.

> (*They go out*)

SECOND STRANGER.

You going in?

RALPH ARDSLEY.

I've got to find a man.

> (*The stranger goes out*)

> (*Ardsley calls toward the room, forward left*)

What's the news from the mill, Charles?

BUTLER.

> (*Appears at the door*)

I haven't heard, sir.
You reckon they'll go back, sir?

RALPH ARDSLEY.

Sure. Where's Gladys?

> (*The Butler walks back toward the conservatory*)

Just tell her I asked about her.

BUTLER.

Yes, sir.

RALPH ARDSLEY.

Thank you.

(*He goes into the room, forward right. The Butler returns to the opposite room. All the people have now withdrawn with the exception of Mrs. Orr, who has come in, centre right, and who lingers about as though she were listening to the upper part of the walls. Later, Mrs. Egerton re-enters, forward right, and glances back into the room from which she has come, to satisfy herself that her guests are occupied. Seeing her, Mrs. Orr comes forward, shaking her head*)

MRS. EGERTON.

No?

MRS. ORR.

No.

MRS. EGERTON.

Nothing at all?

MRS. ORR.

Nothing at all.

MRS. EGERTON.

I never have been sure myself. Sometimes
I've thought I heard it.

MRS. ORR.

I can understand
How one could easily imagine it.

MRS. EGERTON.

If you could be here when the house is still,
Alone— —

MRS. ORR.

> In certain moods, perhaps I should.
> For certainly the trees seem most alive.
> I never would have thought it possible
> To make a forest live and life go on
> In wood as it does here. 'Tis wonderful.

> *(Mrs. Egerton glances across into the room, forward right, from which*
> *comes a sound of merriment)*

MRS. ORR.

> The very squirrels upon the limbs—see there,
> The young one with the pine cone in its mouth.
> And the faint far-awayness of the wood.

MRS. EGERTON.

> *(Confidentially)*

> Sylvia——

MRS. ORR.

> Just now as the couple passed
> Practising, I overheard the girl,
> 'It almost seems the real pines are here
> Dropping their needles on us while we dance.
> As Lillian says, you feel them in your hair.'
> Now, to my way of thinking, it would be
> Far easier to hear the pine trees sigh
> Than feel the needles.

MRS. EGERTON.

> It was not the pines.

MRS. ORR.

> You said a sighing.

> *(Mrs. Egerton says something to her)*

> Why, Mary Egerton!
> How horrible!

MRS. EGERTON.

> It worries me at times.

MRS. ORR.

> You do not mean it! And the house just built!
> You foolish dear.

Mrs. Egerton.

> I know.

Mrs. Orr.

> (*Aside*)
>
> How horrible!

Mrs. Egerton.

> Harry has always been a strange, strange boy;
> So different from the rest. What is it you hear?

Mrs. Orr.

> Why, nothing, nothing at all. My dear, this is
> Really ridiculous. If it were old
> And there were cobwebs here and musty walls
> And rumors had come down of some old crime
> But with the timber, every stick of it
> Fresh from the forest, you might almost say
> Picked from your very garden, a pure bloom,
> Fashioned and shaped by your own husband's hand:
> How any one could fancy such a thing
> Is past my comprehension.
>
>   (*A medley of voices is heard, forward right*)

Mrs. Egerton.

> Here they come.

A Voice.

> Cover his eyes, some of you.

Mrs. Egerton.

> Let's not be seen.
>
>   (*She starts back for the door, centre right*)

Mrs. Orr.

> But we can't talk in there.

Mrs. Egerton.

> I'll slip away.
>
> (*They go out centre right. Amid laughter and a confusion of voices Ralph Ardsley and a fellow-townsman enter forward right leading Governor Braddock, whose eyes are blindfolded. Following these come Donald Egerton, General Chadbourne, Bishop Hardbrooke, members of the Governor's staff in uniform, and other guests*)

GOVERNOR BRADDOCK.

You'll pay for this, gentlemen, you'll pay for this.

RALPH ARDSLEY.

Further, Great Master?

> (*Egerton points back toward the centre of the hall. Himself and the group about him remain more in the foreground*)

EGERTON.

That will do.

> (*They remove the handkerchief from the Governor's eyes*)

GOVERNOR BRADDOCK.

Hi yi!

RALPH ARDSLEY.

You see you wake in Paradise.

FIRST GUEST.

Didn't expect it?

> (*Laughter*)

BISHOP HARDBROOKE.

Your incorruptible administration.

FIRST STAFF MEMBER.

You mean to tell us that you planned all this?

EGERTON.

No, I conceived it, Weston; it's alive
As I hope to show you. But more of that anon.

> (*Calls back to the Governor*)

Does it meet your expectations?

STAFF MEMBERS.

> (*Who have gone rear*)

Splendid! Splendid!

FELLOW-TOWNSMAN.

And in the second story he's got his mill.

SECOND STAFF MEMBER.

> (*To Egerton*)

You don't have strikes up there?

GOVERNOR BRADDOCK.

Well, Egerton,
This is the grandest thing I ever saw.

EGERTON.

I made my mind up, Braddock, years ago
That when I'd sawed my fortune out of lumber
I'd build a mansion where a man could see
Just how I'd done it, starting with the raw,
The standing timber, every phase of it;
A sort of record of these busy times:
For they won't last forever, these great days.

GENERAL CHADBOURNE.

We never see the giants till they're gone.

BISHOP HARDBROOKE.

The day will come when we'll appreciate them.

RALPH ARDSLEY.

Three cheers for one of them.

GUESTS.

Hurrah! Hurrah!

EGERTON.

(*Goes back a little, the group following him, and points right rear*)

Back there you see the swamper clearing brush,
Man's first assault upon primeval forests.
And then the feller with his broader stroke
Hewing a way for apple trees and cities,
And incidentally moving on himself.
And here you see my teams. And, by the way,
They talk of how the horse has followed man
In his march across the ages, but the tree
That sheltered the lost saurian, think of that!

GOVERNOR BRADDOCK.

You must have been a tree in some past life;
You seem to love them so and understand them.

EGERTON.

There's nothing in this world so beautiful

As a pine forest, gentlemen, just at dawn;
The infant breathing of a million needles.
It's like our organ, Bishop, those soft tones.

(Comes forward)

BISHOP HARDBROOKE.

He ought to have lived in old cathedral days.

EGERTON.

And here the rising rollways; then the drive,
The river man.

(Points across left)

GOVERNOR BRADDOCK.

Come out to get a view,
A broader view.

THIRD STAFF MEMBER.

You had men pose for this?

EGERTON.

I'm following the tree.

FOURTH STAFF MEMBER.

That fellow's face.

EGERTON.

These 'broader views' don't interest me much.

GOVERNOR BRADDOCK.

And you think this idea's capable of extension?

EGERTON.

How do you mean?

GENERAL CHADBOURNE.

*(Returning from a word with the Butler, to Ardsley who comes to meet
him)*

I don't see what's the matter.

GOVERNOR BRADDOCK.

A while ago you said — —

RALPH ARDSLEY.

O it's all right.

GOVERNOR BRADDOCK.

You were the first Captain of Industry
In all America to build a house.
That has a meaning in it.

EGERTON.

That's what I said;
That has the least relation to the land.

RALPH ARDSLEY.

This snow you'll see will bring them to their senses.

GOVERNOR BRADDOCK.

Suppose you'd made your fortune out of copper?

FIRST STAFF MEMBER.

Yes, we all build our houses out of timber.

SECOND STAFF MEMBER.

Or cotton?

GUESTS.

Ha, ha, ha!

RALPH ARDSLEY.

Or oil?

SEVERAL.

Yes.

RALPH ARDSLEY.

How would you spiritualize the oil business?

EGERTON.

Ardsley here wants to quote me in his paper.

GENERAL CHADBOURNE.

The Lumber King upon the late decision.

EGERTON.

It's Art, not rebates, that I'm speaking of.
Couldn't I show my derricks on the walls?
And back there red-skins striking fire from flint?

Then our forefathers with their tallow-dips
Watching the easy drills slip up and down?
The tanks here—Ah, you laugh, you dilettanti.
I'll tell you gentlemen what the trouble is:
You're frightened by our natural resources,
And you despise the life of your own land,
The crude, tremendous life we're living here.
The force is too much for you. You want polish.
O I can prove it to you.

RALPH ARDSLEY.

Now you'll get it.

EGERTON.

Yes, Braddock, there's that Capitol Commission.
I'd be ashamed.

GOVERNOR BRADDOCK.

I knew 'twould come.

EGERTON.

And we
Breathing the electric air of this great West,
As rich in life as timber, herds and hops,
Wheat fields and mines, and all these things to be
Raised and translated by the brains of men.
Think of a State dotted with lumber camps
And buzzing day and night with saws and saws,
And as far as the North Pole from old world customs,
Wearing a capitol with Grecian columns
With an old Roman Justice on her comb!
You'd scorn to come here in a gaberdine
Made by some dago in the days of Pompey.
And yet you dress the State up in these things.
No independence.

RALPH ARDSLEY.

Governor?

FIRST STAFF MEMBER.

Call the troops!

EGERTON.

I'd rather cut the timber of this land
And coin its spirit in a thing like this
Than be a Roman Cæsar.

RALPH ARDSLEY.

> Hip hurrah!
> That's what I call a fellow countryman.

BISHOP HARDBROOKE.

> You see we're all Americans down here.

SECOND STAFF MEMBER.

> Now, Governor Braddock, show your stars and stripes.

GOVERNOR BRADDOCK.

> Yet you don't seem to dwell in unity.
> I recollect, and it's not years ago,
> Receiving a petition, and a large one—
> Some six or seven thousand?

THIRD STAFF MEMBER.

> About that.

GOVERNOR BRADDOCK.

> Demanding a withdrawal of some troops.

BISHOP HARDBROOKE.

> We're not responsible for our lower classes.

EGERTON.

> *(Significantly)*
>
> You didn't withdraw them.
>
> *(An embarrassing silence)*

RALPH ARDSLEY.

> *(Slaps the Governor on the shoulder)*
>
> Good American!

FOURTH STAFF MEMBER.

> *(To Bishop Hardbrooke)*
>
> Jesus of Nazareth was a foreigner.

GOVERNOR BRADDOCK.

> The Bishop would hardly say so though.

BISHOP HARDBROOKE.

> And you,
> You, Governor, do you go before the people

With all you know? No secrets, not a one?

GOVERNOR BRADDOCK.

O I'm not saying.

EGERTON.

Editor Ardsley?

RALPH ARDSLEY.

Here.

BISHOP HARDBROOKE.

It eases the heart, brother, to confess.

RALPH ARDSLEY.

It's my stockholders, Bishop.

(*Points to Egerton*)

EGERTON.

General Chadbourne?

GENERAL CHADBOURNE.

I, Colonel, get my orders from above.

(*Points to the Governor*)

GOVERNOR BRADDOCK.

We all do.

(*Points to Egerton*)

RALPH ARDSLEY.

Egerton?

EGERTON.

Then come along.
I've got some good Americans up here
Who don't send in petitions.

GOVERNOR BRADDOCK.

A model mill.

FIRST STAFF MEMBER.

Non-Union?

RALPH ARDSLEY.

They're united in the walls.

> *(Laughter)*

EGERTON.

> *(As they start for the stairs)*

Never you mind, gentlemen, 'twill not be long
Until the model that I've built up here
Will be the model everywhere.

GUESTS.

> *(Led by Ralph Ardsley)*

Hurray!

> *(Attracted by the shouting, some ladies look in, forward right)*

A LADY.

They do have such good times.

> *(They withdraw)*

GENERAL CHADBOURNE.

> *(From the steps to the Butler)*

I'll be upstairs.

*(Seeing the hall empty, the young people who have looked in occasional-
ly from the conservatory, enter and take possession)*

RALPH ARDSLEY.

> *(From the landing)*

Hello, Gladys!

GLADYS EGERTON.

Hello, Ardsley!

RALPH ARDSLEY.

> *(Touching his throat)*

Stunning.

GLADYS EGERTON.

Thank you.

> *(Ardsley disappears after the others. Mrs. Orr enters, forward right,
> and is later joined by Mrs. Egerton)*

MRS. ORR.

You surely have not spoken of this to him?

Mrs. Egerton.

The other night I started to.

Mrs. Orr.

How could you!

(*Mrs. Egerton glances back uneasily into the room*)

Mrs. Orr.

They're all right. Let's go here behind the pines.

Mrs. Egerton

(*Beckons to the Butler*)

Serve them the lunch now, Charles.

(*The Butler goes into the room, forward right. The two women pass left, where they are somewhat shut in by the pines*)

Mrs. Orr.

What did he say?

Mrs. Egerton

And then—I don't know—something in his face—
Perhaps the wonder that I knew would come
That such a thing—If people only knew—
Donald is not the hard unfeeling man—
And knowing this— —

(*She hesitates*)

Mrs. Orr.

And knowing what, my dear?

Mrs. Egerton.

My heart rose up and I—I simply said
That Harry had heard a sighing from the walls.
I told him so much, for it's worried me.
And he at once— —

Mrs. Orr.

(*With spirit*)

I know. 'The pines!'

Mrs. Egerton.

'The pines!'

Mrs. Orr.

I knew it!

Mrs. Egerton.

'The pines!' And walked the floor and laughed;
And such a heart-free laugh I have not heard
In twenty years. 'The pines!'

Mrs. Orr.

'The pines!' Of course.

Mrs. Egerton.

Feeling— —

Mrs. Orr.

Yes, yes!

Mrs. Egerton.

He had caught the very soul
Of the forest.

Mrs. Orr.

And the triumph of it all!

Mrs. Egerton.

Ah, no one knows how many, many years
Donald has dreamed of this, how all his thought
And all his— —

    (*Stands regarding the young people dancing*)

Mrs. Orr.

One has but to look at it.

Mrs. Egerton.

Yet not for it as his, not that at all,
But for the building of it.

Mrs. Orr.

Of course.

Mrs. Egerton.

And now
That it has taken form you cannot think
How like a boy he is, how eagerly
He flees here from the business of the day
And how he walks about enjoying it.

'Tis like the sea. When he is here alone
The burden of his great business falls away
And he is young again. I sometimes feel,
Lying in bed at night and knowing he
Is walking here alone, the lights turned low,
And listening for the sighing of the pines,
That somehow 'tis a woman he has made
And that she whispers to him in these hours,
Comes to him beautiful from out the pines
After his long, long wooing of her— —

Mrs. Orr.

I see!
Beautiful, beautiful! I see! I see!
It needed that one breath to make it live.

Mrs. Egerton.

To Donald, yes.

Mrs. Orr.

Before it was a house,
And now a living thing. I see! I see!

(Kisses the little pines)

Mrs. Egerton.

If one could only know it is not God
Whispering through the walls of our new home
Some dreadful word, and yet with voice so low.

Mrs. Orr.

My dear, your words are perfect Greek to me.

Mrs. Egerton.

You know they say the men are suffering so.
And Donald does not seem to see.

Mrs. Orr.

(Vaguely)

The men?

Mrs. Egerton.

Yes; Harry says that some are without bread.
And we here—and the music and the lights.

Mrs. Orr.

(*In utter astonishment*)

Why, Mary Egerton! You do not mean—
You cannot mean that that suggested this,
That vulgar thing, this beautiful idea!

MRS. EGERTON.

If one could only help them, only help them!

MRS. ORR.

The hunger of a lot of stupid men
Who wish to tell your husband what to do,
And he with a brain like this, and they with claws!

MRS. EGERTON.

It all depends upon such little things,
Things that we've never earned——

MRS. ORR.

(*Mysteriously*)

Harry, you say?

MRS. EGERTON.

That fall right at our feet we don't know how.
The chance of birth! What right have I to this
Who've never done one thing to help the world,
While they who work their lives out——

MRS. ORR.

'Help the world!'

MRS. EGERTON.

Can't even have the food and clothes they need.
People have asked me why—that's why it is
I've done my shopping in the city lately.
You meet them in the stores and on the streets.
And they're so thin, so worn with the long strike.
Just think of children crying for mere bread!
It's horrible. I thought this afternoon
As I stood at the window looking out—
Through the first snow the motor cars came up.
I don't believe they even noticed it.
It means so little to them. It's just snow.
But in the workers' homes—I just can't think
Of God as looking down with unconcern.
I couldn't love Him if I thought He could.

MRS. ORR.

> I don't know what we're ever going to do.

MRS. EGERTON.

> If only some strong, gifted man would come
> And show us how, show us all how to live.
> We'd all be so much happier than we are.

MRS. ORR.

> I wish to goodness I could shut my ears
> And never hear that 'Help the world' again.
> You can't pick up a book or magazine,
> Even a fashion journal, or go out
> To see your friends, it seems— —
>
> *(The men are seen coming down the stairs, the Governor and the Bishop on either side of Egerton. They are all laughing and having a good time)*

MRS. EGERTON.

> I'm very sorry.
> It isn't the place. But I've been so distraught.
> Let us go in and put it all away.
> And you must never mention it. I can't bear
> To think of people talking.

MRS. ORR.

> Hear them laugh!
> I wouldn't live with such a wicked man.

MRS. EGERTON.

> That isn't kind in you.

MRS. ORR.

> In twenty years
> We'll all be wearing grave-clothes.

MRS. EGERTON.

> Sylvia!

MRS. ORR.

> There'll not be one retreat where we can go,
> We ladies of the *ancien régime;*
> We'll all be out, with not a single place
> Where we can make the tables ring with cards
> And laugh and just be gay. Even the pines,

The beautiful pines, are tainted, and the snow.
The winter long I'll never dare go out.
I'll be afraid I'll catch this 'Help the world'
And come home hearing things. You precious goose!
You just shan't give way to this silly mood.
And at the moment when you have about you
The money and the best names in the State;
Just everything that mortal heart can wish.

> *(They watch the men coming down the steps)*

You ought to be so proud.

MRS. EGERTON.

I am.

> *(The piano stops)*

A GIRL.

> *(Who has been waltzing)*

O pshaw!

MRS. ORR.

Even the Governor—don't you see, when he's with Donald
And when his wife's with you, how they both show
How all they are and all they hope to be
They owe to Donald?

MRS. EGERTON.

I know, I know.

A YOUNG MAN.

Come on!

MRS. EGERTON.

And he's so good, so good in many ways.

> *(The young people make for the conservatory)*

MRS. ORR.

And yet so gay, so sensible with it all.

MRS. EGERTON.

It isn't that I'm ungrateful, Sylvia.
I'm never done with thanking God for all
The blessings that I have.

MRS. ORR.

Children and wealth.

Mrs. Egerton.

And Donald, too.

Mrs. Orr.

O really!

A Young Man.

Bring the score!

Mrs. Egerton.

I can't help wishing, though, that he would see
And do for others as he does for us.

(*They stand listening*)

Egerton.

Just let your minds go out about the mountains.

(*A pause*)

Have you had too much punch, or what's the trouble?

(*Laughter*)

Mrs. Orr.

Just hear how joyous hearted! Promise me— —

Mrs. Egerton.

(*In alarm*)

He's telling them of the pines!

Mrs. Orr.

What would you do?

Mrs. Egerton.

(*Beckons to the Butler, who is passing*)

Tell Donald that I wish to speak with— —

Mrs. Orr.

Stop!

Egerton.

It's something, gentlemen, that we all have need of.

Mrs. Orr.

Dear, if you ever dare tell Donald this
And pass this ghastly whisper to his heart,
I'll be the Secret Lady of the Pines;
I'll whisper something. What if Donald knew
Who's kept the strike afoot? The great unknown
Contributor to the Citizens' Relief?
Who had twelve hundred dollars in the bank,
A present from a Christmas long ago?
Twelve hundred and twelve hundred— —!

Mrs. Egerton.

It can't be!

Mrs. Orr.

We bankers' wives— —

Mrs. Egerton.

A mere coincidence.

Mrs. Orr.

It's not; he's checked it out. So! If you care
Nothing for Donald's happiness, I do.

(*She leaves Mrs. Egerton standing near the pines. Other ladies have
begun to come in*)

Ralph Ardsley.

What's underneath the forest?

Mrs. Orr.

(*With a strange smile, calling back*)

I really will.

Egerton.

You give it up?

Mrs. Egerton.

My noble, noble son!

General Chadbourne.

He's waiting, gentlemen, till he finds the mine.

Egerton.

The man of parts!

Several.

Of course.

EGERTON.

> That's why I can't
> Take you down now. But when I find the mine
> And get the gold to puddling in the pots,
> If I can find me plastic metal workers
> That I can mould and hammer while they mould
> And hammer out my vision on the walls,
> I'll show you through some subterranean chambers
> Will set your eyes a-dazzle. In the dark,
> Lit by the torches in the miners' caps,
> You'll see the world of metals moving up
> Through human hands as here you see the tree.
> That's why my basement isn't finished yet.

CRIES.

Good luck! Good luck!

EGERTON.

I hope you'll be alive.

> *(He leaves the group and comes forward)*

GOVERNOR BRADDOCK.

Magnificent conception.

BISHOP HARDBROOKE.

A great man.

EGERTON.

> *(To the Butler)*

Call them in, Charles. Have all of them come in.

GOVERNOR BRADDOCK.

Metals, then trees, then mills, then books and pictures.

BISHOP HARDBROOKE.

Raw matter on its spiral up to spirit.

EGERTON.

While we're at riddles, gentlemen — —

> *(Ladies come in, centre and forward right)*

EGERTON.

Come right in.
If you'll allow me, friends, suppose you stand
Where you can have my forest in your eye.

(He arranges them to face right)

I don't see, ladies, how you ever endure
The dulness of these males. We've been at riddles.
Come in. I've kept my best wine for the last.

(He steps back near the door, centre right)

Suppose you'd made an Adam out of clay,
Worked years to get it to your satisfaction,
And now you're looking at it, hands all washed
And mind confronting, weighing what's been done.
Suddenly you're aware of something standing by you
That whispers in your left ear: 'Make a wish
Within the power of God.' What would it be?

Bishop Hardbrooke.

To see it walk about the garden, brother.

Egerton.

Suppose your Adam was a pine-wood, Bishop,
That couldn't walk.

Mrs. Orr.

(Ardently)

Then just to hear it breathe.

Egerton.

A woman's intuition!

(Looks to see who it is)

Sylvia Orr!

Bishop Hardbrooke.

Sylva a forest.

Egerton.

An old friend of mine.

(He gives a signal to some one)

A clear day in the pine-wood.

(Suddenly the hall is beautifully illuminated)

Guests.

Ah!

EGERTON.

With clouds,
The dawn just breaking.

(*The hall becomes gray and shadowy*)

Ancient silence.

MRS. EGERTON.

(*Half in terror*)

Donald!

EGERTON.

Let us be quiet now.

(*The silence is broken by the ringing of a telephone bell in the room
forward left*)

GENERAL CHADBOURNE.

Ah!

MRS. ORR.

(*Across to Mrs. Egerton*)

Don't you dare!

(*The Butler goes out to answer the telephone*)

GOVERNOR BRADDOCK.

This age of bells and whistles.

GENERAL CHADBOURNE.

(*Comes forward and takes his stand near the door forward left*)

Just in time!

EGERTON.

They don't concern me. We are far away
With quiet all about us and the woods.

(*The silence is intense*)

GENERAL CHADBOURNE.

(*Rehearsing his speech*)

... And it gives me pleasure to announce to you
Upon the occasion of the opening
Of your new mansion, Colonel Egerton,

This bit of news, sir, from the military;
And I offer it with our congratulations:
The strike is over;
The men have yielded and have gone to work.
And all's been done without one— —

> (*Enter the Butler hurriedly*)

GENERAL CHADBOURNE.

Here I am.

BUTLER.

> (*Passing him*)

For Mr. Egerton.

GENERAL CHADBOURNE.

No!

BUTLER.

> (*In a low voice over the crowd*)

Mr. Egerton!

GENERAL CHADBOURNE.

Isn't that Captain Haskell?

BUTLER.

Mr. Jergens.

> (*Egerton comes forward, making his way through the crowd*)

GENERAL CHADBOURNE.

Butler!

> (*The Butler goes to him and they talk*)

RALPH ARDSLEY.

> (*Calls after Egerton as he goes out left*)

Good luck!

> (*Calls to Chadbourne*)

This probably ends it.

GOVERNOR BRADDOCK.

What's your opinion of these mysteries, Bishop?

BISHOP HARDBROOKE.

I'm one of those that simply stand and wait.

GOVERNOR BRADDOCK.

You don't believe in modern miracles.

BISHOP HARDBROOKE.

There are miracles and miracles, Governor Braddock.
I try to keep elastic in these things,
Steering a middle course with open mind.

RALPH ARDSLEY.

(Calls to Chadbourne)

Needed just this to crown the time we're having.

BISHOP HARDBROOKE.

We are living in an age in many ways
Without a parallel. I sometimes think—
If I may say it not too seriously—
Of those last days we read of when the world
Goes on its way unconscious of the end.
We give and take in marriage, eat and drink,
And meet our friends in social intercourse,
And all the while a Spirit walks beside us,
Enters our homes and writes upon our walls.
There are whispers everywhere if we could hear them;
And some of them grow louder with the days;
And pools of quiet ruffle and show storms.
You, Governor, feel the popular unrest
As it manifests itself in politics,
The shift of parties and of principles,
Rocks that we used to think would never change.
And brother Egerton in industry;
He feels it.

EGERTON.

*(Appearing at the door, excited, and keeping back so as not to be seen
by the people)*

Chadbourne!

(The General joins him and they disappear)

BISHOP HARDBROOKE.

I sincerely hope
We're on the eve, however, of a day
When trouble-makers in the ranks of Labor,
Not only here in Foreston but elsewhere,
May find it to their interest to respect,

Nay, reverence as a thing ordained by God,
The right of men to earn their daily bread,
As well as profitable to obey the laws
Without the unseemly presence of armed men.

(*There is a clapping of hands. General Chadbourne appears just inside the door and beckons to Ardsley, who goes in to him*)

BISHOP HARDBROOKE.

And I will take occasion here and now
To say what you've been thinking all this while,
And in the presence of the man himself:
We are fortunate, my friends — —

RALPH ARDSLEY.

(*Appears and calls to one of the guests farther back*)
The Governor.

BISHOP HARDBROOKE.

In having at the helm of our great State
One who loves order more than he loves votes.

(*General clapping of hands*)

SEVERAL.

Good!

GUEST.

(*In a low voice over the crowd*)
Governor!

SEVERAL.

That's good!

(*The Governor bows*)

CRIES.

Speech! Speech!

GOVERNOR BRADDOCK.

My friends,
I quite agree with the Bishop.

SEVERAL.

Ha, ha, ha!

GOVERNOR BRADDOCK.

I don't mean in his estimate of me.

(*More laughter. The Governor catches sight of the guest beckoning to him*)

GOVERNOR BRADDOCK.

But here's my better half. You might ask her.
Pardon me till I see— —

RALPH ARDSLEY.

(*Calls urgently to the Bishop in a voice that is barely heard*)

Go on! Go on!

BISHOP HARDBROOKE.

Society, my friends, is like this house,
This mansion that we all so much admire.

(*Ardsley stands impassive till the Governor has gone out and the Bishop has again got the attention of the people, then goes quickly into the side room*)

BISHOP HARDBROOKE.

Imagine what a state of things we'd have
If every wooden fellow in these walls,
Not only here but in the mill upstairs,
Should lend his heart to tongues of discontent
Until his very tools became a burden.

A VOICE.

Anarchy.

BISHOP HARDBROOKE.

Very true. Where would this be,
This beautiful thing that Colonel Egerton
Has built with so much labor and so much taste?
And out there in the world where we all dwell,
Where all of us have places in the walls,
Some working with their hands on farms, in mines;
Some building; some at forges; at machines
Weaving our garments; others more endowed
Loaned to us from the higher planes of being,
Men of the Over-Soul, inventors, dreamers,
Planners of longer railroads, bigger mills,
The great preparers for the finer souls
That build the dome, the finishers of things,
Prophets of God, musicians, artists, poets,
As we've all seen how Colonel Egerton

In his third story has his books and pictures—
Suppose a bitter wind of discontent
Should shake the great walls of this social order,
Set the first story men against the second,
The second against the third, until the mass,
Throwing their tools down on the world's great floor,
Should clamor up the dome for pens and brushes,
Shutting their eyes to the cold facts of life
That we climb up Life's ladder by degrees—

(His attention is attracted for a moment to a group of men that has been collecting forward centre, evidently concerned with whatever it is that is going on in the side room)

BISHOP HARDBROOKE.

(Recovering himself quickly)

But I'm afraid, my friends— —

SEVERAL.

Go on! Go on!

BISHOP HARDBROOKE.

I'm wasting good material for a sermon.

A MAN'S VOICE.

Pearls before swine.

BISHOP HARDBROOKE.

I started to say brethren.

(Laughter)

A LADY.

(In the foreground)

Isn't he just too bright for anything!

BISHOP HARDBROOKE.

But now— —

A MAN.

(Joining the group)

What's up?

BISHOP HARDBROOKE.

To come home to the task
That brother Egerton lays upon our ears.

We have all of us read stories and seen things.

(*Laughter*)

A Voice.

But ghosts of trees?

(*General laughter*)

Bishop Hardbrooke.

That, I admit, is rare.

(*Mrs. Egerton, who, since the ringing of the telephone bell, has shown an increasing anxiety as to the message that has come, unable longer to contain herself, comes hurriedly forward through the people*)

Bishop Hardbrooke.

Don't let us scare you, sister Egerton.

(*Laughter. The people turn just in time to see Governor Braddock, General Chadbourne, and Ralph Ardsley with overcoats on and hats in their hands, stealing across to get out forward right. Mrs. Egerton hurries into the room from which they came*)

Ralph Ardsley.

It's nothing.

(*The three go out*)

Voices.

What's the matter? What's the matter?

Pale Lady.

It's something terrible, I know it is.

Lady in Black.

We always have to pay for our good times.

(*George Egerton and Gladys Egerton come quickly from the conservatory and enter the side room*)

Elderly Lady.

I shouldn't wonder if those horrid strikers
Were burning the mill.

Lady in Black.

Or may be some one's hurt.

Lady With the Conspicuous Coiffure.

Provoking, isn't it?

FAT LADY.

What would we better do?

YOUNG MATRON.

> (*Calling out*)

Please tell us what's the trouble.

> (*A silence*)

PALE LADY.

I shall faint.

BISHOP HARDBROOKE.

> (*Coming forward*)

It has been suggested, friends, in view of this
Personal something that has happened here—
I don't know what it is, but we all know
In trouble how we like to be alone.
Later I'll call them up and for us all
Extend our sympathy when we know the cause.

> (*There is a movement of people departing*)

PINK LADY.

I wonder who it is?

FAT LADY.

They've shut the door.

LADY WITH THE CONSPICUOUS COIFFURE.

'Twas more like anger; didn't you see his face?

LADY IN BLACK.

When everything was so, so beautiful!

> (*They vanish with the other guests. A minute or so later the Butler
> enters, right rear, and walks as though dazed through the empty hall*)

A MAID.

> (*Appearing right rear*)

Charlie!

SECOND MAID.

> (*Appears beside her*)

What is it?

BUTLER.

(*Without turning*)

Trouble at the mill.

FIRST MAID.

Charlie!

BUTLER.

That's all I know.

SECOND MAID.

A riot?

GLADYS EGERTON.

(*Appearing forward left*)

Gone!
Father, they've gone!

GEORGE EGERTON.

(*Comes in quickly*)

Look in the rooms.

(*Goes rear*)

GLADYS EGERTON.

(*Looks in the room forward right*)

They've gone!

GEORGE EGERTON.

(*Calls into the conservatory*)

Chester! Marjorie! Well, I'll be damned!

GLADYS EGERTON.

I hate him, O I hate him!

GEORGE EGERTON.

That's what comes!

GLADYS EGERTON.

What will we ever do! Just think of it!

GEORGE EGERTON.

> *(To the Butler)*

Why do you stand that way?

> *(Comes to the door forward left)*

O do shut up,
Mother.

> *(Donald Egerton comes in, putting on his overcoat)*

MRS. EGERTON.

> *(Following him)*

Remember, Donald, he's our son.

GEORGE EGERTON.

Always defending him! You make me sick.

MRS. EGERTON.

You've always said you never in your life
Lost hold upon yourself.

GLADYS EGERTON.

No dance to-night.

EGERTON.

> *(To the Butler)*

Tell Jack to bring the car to the front door.

> *(The Butler goes out centre right)*

GEORGE EGERTON.

Wait, father, till I get my— —

> *(Starts for the room forward left)*

MRS. EGERTON.

If he's done it—
He has some reason, Donald. And you know
Jergens has never liked him.

> *(Harry Egerton comes in right rear, his hat and shoulders covered with snow)*

MRS. EGERTON.

Harry! Harry!

> *(She hurries to him and embraces him)*

HARRY EGERTON.

Mother!

MRS. EGERTON.

My son!

HARRY EGERTON.

I'm sorry.

(*George Egerton reappears*)

GLADYS EGERTON.

I just hate you!
You selfish thing! See what you've done!

HARRY EGERTON.

I'm sorry.

GEORGE EGERTON.

(*With a sneer*)

He's very sorry, sister.

EGERTON.

A pretty son!

HARRY EGERTON.

I hadn't the least intention, father— —

GEORGE EGERTON.

Damn you!

HARRY EGERTON.

Who 'phoned it in?

MRS. EGERTON.

What is it you've done, Harry?

GEORGE EGERTON.

(*To the Butler and the Maids who have appeared at the doors*)

Get away from there!

HARRY EGERTON.

Father— —

(*Egerton Tosses His Overcoat Into the Side Room*)

MRS. EGERTON.

Harry, is it true
You kept the men from going back to work?

HARRY EGERTON.

I wanted to have a talk with father first.

EGERTON.

Um!

GEORGE EGERTON.

(*To his mother*)

There!

MRS. EGERTON.

But hear him, Donald.

HARRY EGERTON.

All my life
I've wanted to say something to you, father;
Especially since I went to work. You once,
When I came home from college, you remember,
And hadn't made my mind up what to do,
What my life work should be——

EGERTON.

A pretty son!

HARRY EGERTON.

We talked together and you said that now
Three things lay open to me, that I could choose
And that you'd back me up. First, there was Art.
And though you didn't say so, I could see
You'd have been glad if I had chosen that.
I had a talent for it, so you said,
And I could study with the best of them.
You'd set aside a hundred thousand dollars;
And I could finish up by travelling,
Seeing the beautiful buildings of the world;
That I could take my time, then settle down
And glorify my land: that's what you said.
Then there was Public Life. You'd start me in
By giving me the Courier. That, you said,
Would give me at once a standing among men
And training in political affairs.
And that if I made good you'd see to it

I had a seat in Congress, and in the end
That probably I'd be Governor of the State.
And then you paused. You didn't like the third.
Business, you said, was an unpleasant life.
'Twas all right as you'd used it, as a means,
But as an end—And then you used words, father,
That changed my life although you didn't know it—
'Business, my son, is war; needful at times,
But as a life,—you shook your head and sighed.
With that we ended it, for some one came
And I went out. Six years ago last June,
The seventh of June; I can't forget the day.
The sun was shining but a strange new light
Lay over everything. All of a sudden
It dawned upon my mind that I'd been reared
Inside a garden full of flowers and trees,
And only now had chanced upon the gate
And stepped out. There was smoke upon the skies
And a rumbling of strange wagons in the street.
I was afraid. For every man I met
Seemed just about to ask, 'What side are you on?'
And I was twenty-one and didn't know.

Egerton.

You seem to have found out since you've been away.

Harry Egerton.

I'd always thought 'twas garden everywhere.
I walked on up the river and sat down
Upon the logs up there, and night came on.
And in the waters flowing at my feet
The lighted land went by, cities and towns
And the vast murmur and the daily life
Of those that toil, the hunger and the care.
And in my heart I knew that it was true,
That what you said was true. And I came back
Filled with such peace as I had never known.
'I'll enter business, father.' And I did.
I started at the bottom in the mill
Helping the engineer, and from the saws
Carried the lumber with the other men.
Then in the yard. You always praised my work.
I'm in the office now at twenty-seven,
And Secretary of the Company.
I think I know the business pretty well.
You've said so. But somehow——

(*He pauses*)

Mrs. Egerton.

What is it, Harry?

Harry Egerton.

In Public Life, if I had chosen that,
And after six years' work that you approved,
If one day I had come— —

Egerton.

You want the mill.

Harry Egerton.

'Father, I can't go on; my way is blocked
And all my hopes are falling to the ground.'
There's nothing, not one thing you wouldn't have done.
Or if I had a building half way up,
My masterpiece, a mighty capitol
That finished would be known throughout the land,
And I had met with interference, men
Who had no vision—you know what I mean—
And I had come to you, 'Father, I'm thwarted,'
O I can see with one sweep of your hand
How you would clear the skies.

Egerton.

You want the mill.

Harry Egerton.

Yes, father.

Egerton.

I thought so.

Harry Egerton.

I want the mill.

George Egerton.

And thought you'd blackmail father.

Harry Egerton.

Listen to me!
For probably in all my life I'll never
Speak to you as I'm speaking now, my father.

Mrs. Egerton.

Donald, I beg of you — —

George Egerton.

Well, I'll be — —

Mrs. Egerton.

George!

Harry Egerton.

In these six years for one cause or another
There've been three strikes that have cost the Company thousands
In money, to say nothing of those things
That all the money in the world can't buy.
Now let me ask, my father, if this loss,
Instead of springing from these strikes, had come
Through breakdowns of the machinery, or in the camps
Through failure to get the timber out in time,
Wouldn't you have dismissed the man in charge?
Then why do you let Jergens run the mill?
Hasn't he failed, and miserably, with the men?

George Egerton.

What have you to do with it?

Egerton.

I'll attend to this.

*(George Egerton walks away and stands by the pine trees, picking off
and biting the needles)*

Harry Egerton.

Is it because the earnings have increased?
Think what it's cost you, father. In every mill
Jergens has touched he's left a cursing there
That's all come back on us. Why, my father,
Our name's become a by-word through the State,
'As hard as Egerton.' And when I think
Of what might be, the good-will and the peace,
The happiness! There's not the least excuse
For this cut in wages, father, and you know it.

Egerton.

Um!

Harry Egerton.

You can't help but know it. You've the books;
You know what you've been making. But that aside:
To come to what I would say: You've won this strike.
You have the men in your power and you can say,
'Go back,' and they'll go back. But you won't do it.

EGERTON.

Won't I?

HARRY EGERTON.

Will you, when you know you're wrong?
When you know you're losing friends who love what's right?
Think of the sentiment against you, father.
No, father, you don't know what's going on.

EGERTON.

It seems I don't.

HARRY EGERTON.

If you knew how they live
And the hard time they have to get along.
It isn't fair, my father, it isn't fair.

GLADYS EGERTON.

(In tears, to her mother)

Yes, you don't care.

HARRY EGERTON.

Father, you love this land.
There's never been a day in all your life,
If there'd been war, you wouldn't have closed the mill
And gone and died upon the field of battle
If the country had called to you in her need.
And I can see you how you'd scorn the man,
If he were serving as a General,
Who'd keep his rank and file as poorly fed
And ragged as he could.

(The telephone bell rings)

GLADYS EGERTON.

They're calling up
To know about it!

GEORGE EGERTON.

(Starts for the room, then stops)

What shall I tell them, father?

Gladys Egerton.

O have them come back, papa, have them come back!

Egerton.

(Keeping his eye on Harry)

Tell them what you please.

(George goes out)

Harry Egerton.

Father, buy Jergens out.

Gladys Egerton.

(Calling into the room)

Tell them it's all right, brother, that it's nothing.

Harry Egerton.

Give him his price and let him go his way— —

Egerton.

(Calling toward the room)

A misunderstanding.

Harry Egerton.

And let me run the mill.
And let us see, my father, you and I,
If we can't make that place of work down there
As famous for its harmony as this house.
A land is not its timber but its people,
And not its Art, my father, but its men.
Let's try to make this town a place of peace
And helpfulness. What do you say, my father?

Egerton.

And that's your life work!

(Gladys goes into the room)

Mrs. Egerton.

(Approaching him)

Donald— —

Egerton.

Go away.

MRS. EGERTON.

You've asked me why it is I cannot sleep.
It's that, Donald, it's that! Give him the mill.
They're human beings, Donald, like ourselves.

EGERTON.

And you've been planning this!

HARRY EGERTON.

I had hoped, my father,
That things would so arrange themselves that I—
That you would make me manager of the mill.

MRS. EGERTON.

Donald, it's your nobler self you hear.

EGERTON.

(Looks at him a long time)

What a fool— —

(Turns away)

what a fool I've been!

(Walks about)

VOICES OF GEORGE AND GLADYS.

The mine! Father!

(They come running in)

The mine! A rumor that the mine's been found!

EGERTON.

Who is it?

GEORGE EGERTON.

I don't know. They're on the wire.

(Egerton goes out)

GEORGE EGERTON.

All over town, they say.

(Brother and sister wait near the door, tense, listening)

MRS. EGERTON.

(With a sigh)

Everything!

GLADYS EGERTON.

(*Under her breath*)

George,
Think of the things we'll have!

GEORGE EGERTON.

Be still!

MRS. EGERTON.

(*Turns and looks at Harry, whose face shows the sadness he feels at his
father's refusal*)

Harry.
Harry, are you well?

HARRY EGERTON.

Yes, mother.

(*A pause*)

Mother — —

(*Distant cannon are heard*)

GEORGE EGERTON.

Hark!

GLADYS EGERTON.

(*Starting back through the house*)

The mine! the mine!

(*The servants appear*)

Father has found the mine!

(*Further booming is heard*)

GEORGE EGERTON.

There go the guns! They're celebrating, father!

(*He starts for the stairs and goes bounding up three steps at a time*)

GLADYS EGERTON.

(*Calling after him*)

We'll have them back and announce it! We'll have them back!

HARRY EGERTON.

Mother, I've found the mine.

GLADYS EGERTON.

> *(Whirling round on her toe)*

Now, now you see!

HARRY EGERTON.

This morning on the mountains.

MRS. EGERTON.

Can it be!

GLADYS EGERTON.

> *(Comes running forward)*

I'll have my car now, won't I, daddy, daddy?

> *(She disappears into the room, forward left)*

MRS. EGERTON.

> *(Strangely)*

I knew it! O I knew that He would come!

> *(Turns upon her son a look of awe)*

Harry! Harry!

HARRY EGERTON.

Father must do what's right.

MRS. EGERTON.

You'll build a mill.

HARRY EGERTON.

The ground is white with snow.

> *(Egerton appears in the doorway and stands looking at his son)*

GLADYS EGERTON.

> *(Clinging to his hand)*

What is it, papa? What's the matter, daddy?

GEORGE EGERTON.

> *(Appearing upon the stairs)*

They've run the flag up on the Court House, father!

EGERTON.

That's what it means!

HARRY EGERTON.

Father, I'll buy the mill.

EGERTON.

That's what it means!

GLADYS EGERTON.

What, daddy?

EGERTON.

You'll hold my men!

HARRY EGERTON.

I'll mortgage the mine and pay you, father.

GLADYS EGERTON.

Oh!

EGERTON.

And if I don't you'll back the men, eh?

GLADYS EGERTON.

Oh!

(She backs toward George, who has come down the stairs)

HARRY EGERTON.

I'll pay you twice its value, father.

GEORGE EGERTON.

(At a word from Gladys)

What!

(Egerton drops his eyes for a moment and stands as though in deep thought)

MRS. EGERTON.

Be careful, Donald!

GLADYS EGERTON.

(To Harry)

I hate you!

GEORGE EGERTON.

(With a sneer)

Big man!

EGERTON.

George,
Get Jergens.

GEORGE EGERTON.

(*To Harry*)

Mill-hand!

(*Goes out left*)

EGERTON.

Tell him to lock the mill
And have this notice tacked up on the gate,
'Closed for a year.'

VOICE OF GEORGE.

Good!

GLADYS EGERTON.

Good!

EGERTON.

I'll let her rot.

HARRY EGERTON.

And winter coming on!

GLADYS EGERTON.

I'm glad! I'm glad!

EGERTON.

War or submission, eh?

HARRY EGERTON.

(*Goes to his mother*)

Mother.

(*Kisses her*)

EGERTON.

I'll show you— —

HARRY EGERTON.

(*Starting for the door*)

Father, you'll remember in the years to be
How I came to you one November day
And asked your help to give this country peace.

EGERTON.

Go to your rabble!

GLADYS EGERTON.

(Breaks out crying)

Think of it!

EGERTON.

I'll show you
How you can buy me and my property!

HARRY EGERTON.

(From back in the hall)

Property was made for men.

EGERTON.

And don't you ever
Darken that door!

HARRY EGERTON.

And you can't keep it idle
While men depend upon it for their bread.

(He goes out)

EGERTON.

(Roaring after him)

You dare to lay your hands upon that mill!

(He stands staring at the door)

MRS. EGERTON.

(Wonderingly)

It wasn't our son! It wasn't our son!

(The cannon are heard in volley upon volley as of a town giving itself
up to celebration)

EGERTON.

(Calls into the room, left)

Tell him to go right down, that probably
There'll be an attack upon it.

GLADYS EGERTON.

> (*Shaken with sobs*)

Think of it!

MRS. EGERTON.

> (*As before*)

That gleam about his brow! And now he's gone!

> (*She wanders back in the hall as in a dream*)

EGERTON.

And to see Chadbourne——Are you listening?

VOICE OF GEORGE.

Yes.

EGERTON.

To Chadbourne that he has authority from me—
From Egerton, to treat them all alike.

MRS. EGERTON.

> (*Vacantly, to her husband*)

What have you done, Donald!

EGERTON.

That I expect
The mill defended, let it cost what may.

GLADYS EGERTON.

I hate him, O I hate him!

MRS. EGERTON.

> (*Who has come forward and stands facing him*)

What have you done!

ACT IV

THE LIVING MILL

Scene: Inside the mill, showing in front a sort of half storeroom, half office shut in from the main body of the mill by a railing in the centre of which is a gate that swings in and out. Far back in this main body of the mill one sees a number of great gang saws from which off-carriers, with freshly sawed slabs and lumber upon their rollers, branch right from the main line that runs the full length of the mill. Through an opening in the far end, whence the logs are drawn up an incline to the saws, one sees as through a telescope a portion of the river and of the mountains on the opposite bank. Up toward the front, left, in this main body of the mill is a wide door that opens outside. In the foreground, within the space partitioned off by the railing, a pair of stairs, evidently connecting with the outdoors on the ground floor, comes up rear left. Centre, against this left wall, a pole six or eight inches in diameter, and to all appearances only recently set, goes up through a hole in the roof. Upon the floor at the foot of the pole, from which two long ropes hang down, lies a large American flag partially strung upon the rope. Forward from the pole is a door which apparently is no longer in use, a strip being nailed across it. About this end of the enclosure are piles of window sash and kegs of nails. Centre rear, at right angles to the side walls, so that one sitting upon a stool may look back into the mill, is a long checkers' desk with two or three stools before it and with the usual litter of papers, books, and a telephone upon it. In the right wall, rear, where one coming up the stairs may walk straight on and enter, is a door connecting with the main office.

As the Scene opens, something very important seems to be going on in this main office. A crowd of men, workmen and militiamen together, are packed about the door, intent upon whatever it is that is transpiring inside. Forward, away from the crowd, a small group, mostly of militiamen, is gathered about two guards with rifles in their hands, who have evidently just come in. Back, beyond the railing and close to the crowd, a group of workmen about Wes Dicey is engaged in a heated argument. And farther back in the mill, especially about the large door, left, are bodies of men talking together. As the Scene opens, and for a few minutes afterwards, some one up the pole is heard singing.

Time: Saturday afternoon the week following the preceding Act.

A Workman.

> (*Comes from the crowd to the militiamen*)

Servin' the papers on the mine, you think?

MILITIAMAN.

He's too damn proud to play the constable.

SECOND MILITIAMAN.

Maybe it's terms from Egerton.

THIRD MILITIAMAN.

(*To Fourth Militiaman, who has just come up the stairs with his shoulders hung with knapsacks*)

Chadbourne's here.

SECOND WORKMAN.

Egerton makes no terms till he's on top.

FIFTH MILITIAMAN.

He'll have his hands full. Seen the evening papers?

(*He unfolds a paper and a group gathers about him*)

CRIES.

(*Near the door*)

That's right! that's right!

THIRD WORKMAN.

(*From the edge of the crowd*)

What are they sayin', Mike?

FOURTH WORKMAN.

(*On the edge of the crowd, looking toward the group about Dicey*)

We can't hear nothin' with that racket there.

FIRST MILITIAMAN.

It's his lost sheep he's after.

SECOND MILITIAMAN.

Let him bark.

FOURTH WORKMAN.

You've stood by us, boys, and we'll stand by you.

VOICE.

(*From back in the mill*)

Tell him we won't, no matter what he says!

(*The Sixth Militiaman comes up the stairs, with four or five bugles, and shows surprise to see the crowd gathered)*

THIRD MILITIAMAN.

> *(In the group about the paper)*

And Smith and Balding Brothers!

FOURTH WORKMAN.

Lemme see it.

FIFTH MILITIAMAN.

Give him a rouse. What say you. One, two, three.

SEVERAL.

Hurrah for Harry Egerton! Hurrah!

VOICE.

> *(Rear)*

Hurrah for the Living Mill!

A GENERAL SHOUT.

> *(Back in the mill)*

The Living Mill!

FIFTH MILITIAMAN.

I guess, by God, he knows where we stand now.

> *(They join the crowd about the door. Jim King comes through the gate in the railing, followed by Rome Masters, who is considerably intoxicated)*

JIM KING.

And hug 'em round the neck, if I was you.
That's what I'd do.

ROME MASTERS.

Now you just stop that, Jim.

JIM KING.

Why did you tell Aug. Jergens that you would?

ROME MASTERS.

I ain't said nothin' about backin' down.
But I ain't nothin' agin him.

JIM KING.

There you go!
It does beat hell. You just keep saying that,
That you ain't nothin' agin him, and you'll see.

VOICE.

(*Near the door*)

Who's to be judge what's for the Public Good?

ROME MASTERS.

I ain't said that I wouldn't do the job.

JIM KING.

(*Stands on tip-toe and looks over the crowd, then turns back to Masters*)

Didn't you think and didn't I think and Wes
That when they cut the pie we'd get our share,
One big long table with no head and tail
But all the boys the same, and everything
Piled on it and divided?

(*The group about Dicey become more noisy*)

VOICE.

(*From the crowd*)

Put him out!

(*Dicey comes from the centre of the group and catches sight of King, who beckons to him*)

FIRST WORKMAN.

(*From the group*)

If you don't like it, Wes, why don't you leave?

SECOND WORKMAN.

(*Following Dicey*)

Why in the hell don't you leave? We're free men.

(*Dicey, King and Masters walk over to the pile of sash, left*)

THIRD WORKMAN.

(*Of the Dicey faction*)

Offer 'em coppers for their Union cards.

FOURTH WORKMAN.

And where's the mine that you was goin' to share?

FIFTH WORKMAN.

You want old Egerton to have it, eh?

VOICE.

>   (*Back in the mill*)

Bring on the Constitution and let's vote!

CHRIS KNUDSON.

>   (*Comes out of the crowd*)

Don't use that name.

>   (*To the Dicey faction*)

Let's have no trouble, men.
This ain't no time to quarrel among ourselves.

>   (*To the other party*)

Try to remember, boys, it's his name, too.

(*Suddenly there is a tremendous cheering by those about the door. A militiaman hurries from the crowd, grabs a bugle from the Sixth Militiaman and, darting out centre, starts to blow it*)

SIXTH MILITIAMAN.

>   (*Excitedly*)

Don't do that! Here!

MILITIAMAN.

>   (*With the knapsacks*)

Don't do that!

(*The crowd begins to break up, many of the men climbing back over the railing into the mill proper*)

MILITIAMAN.

>   (*Comes sliding down the pole*)

What's the trouble?

JIM KING.

>   (*Returning with Dicey and Masters*)

They're out for their selves, damn 'em; we'll be too.

SEVENTH MILITIAMAN.

>   (*Coming away with two or three others*)

Young Egerton's pure gold if ever was.

WES DICEY.

> Don't make no move, though, Jim, till we see first.
>
> *(He separates himself from the other two, and they mingle with the men)*

EIGHTH MILITIAMAN.

> That's just the way they did the old man's farm.
> We had a place and didn't want to sell.
> That made no difference. Eminent Domain.
> 'Out of the way there, home!'

VOICE.

> *(From back in the mill)*
>
> What did he say?

VOICE.

> *(Near the door)*
>
> Then if the Company can take men's lands
> To build their railroads through— —

SECOND VOICE.

> That's a good point!

FIRST VOICE.

> And if you say the Law's the same for all,
> Then why can't we take theirs when we need bread?

FIFTH MILITIAMAN.

> *(Getting a group together)*
>
> Be smoking when he comes out.

FIRST MILITIAMAN.

> Stamper! Kids!

THIRD VOICE.

> *(Rear)*
>
> What Egerton wants, that's for the Public Good!

CHRIS KNUDSON.

> There, there you're not remembering it again!
>
> *(General Chadbourne comes from the office, followed by Captain Haskell, and after these Harry Egerton, Sam Williams, Harvey Anderson, Buck Bentley, and others. The militiamen make a big smoke)*

GENERAL CHADBOURNE.

You'll not lay hands on property in this State.

HARRY EGERTON.

The right of men to work is just as sacred
As is the right of property, General Chadbourne,
And more important to the general welfare.

GENERAL CHADBOURNE.

These gates have stood wide open here for weeks.

SAM WILLIAMS.

And on whose terms?

WORKMEN.

That's the point; on whose terms?

GENERAL CHADBOURNE.

Of course you'd like to make the terms yourselves.

HARVEY ANDERSON.

Why shouldn't they?

HARRY EGERTON.

What would you have men do?

HARVEY ANDERSON.

You say the State's been fair with them. All right.
But it ain't the State that feeds them, it's the Mill;
And it ain't the State that clothes them, it's the Mill;
And it ain't the State they think of when they think
Of better homes hereafter, it's the Mill.
And there ain't no fairness that ain't fair in here,
And there ain't no freedom that ain't free in here,
Though there ain't no use of saying that to you.

SAM WILLIAMS.

We have to live.

GENERAL CHADBOURNE.

(Ignoring Anderson, as he does throughout)

Employers have the right
To buy their labor in the open market,
And if you fellows here can't meet the price— —

VOICE.

> (*From the crowd*)

You'd have us starve?

GENERAL CHADBOURNE.

You'll have to step aside
And give way to some stronger men that can

SAM WILLIAMS.

And you expect men to obey a law
That gives no hope of anything but this?

GENERAL CHADBOURNE.

You'd been to work and you'd been satisfied
If some outsiders hadn't come along
And fired your ignorant minds.

> (*Murmurs in the crowd*)

CHRIS KNUDSON.

Hold your tongues, men.

HARRY EGERTON.

Pardon me, General Chadbourne—

HARVEY ANDERSON.

> (*To Buck Bentley*)

Land o' the free!

HARRY EGERTON.

We are all of us outsiders in a way,
Yourself as well as Harvey here and I.
But in a way there's no such thing. We're men,
And that which injures one injures us all.

GENERAL CHADBOURNE.

I'm here on duty; quite a different thing.

HARRY EGERTON.

What I have done I have done not without cause
Nor hastily.

GENERAL CHADBOURNE.

You know yourself these men
Would have been to work.

Sam Williams.

We'd had to— —

General Chadbourne.

There you are!

Sam Williams.

If it hadn't been for Mr. Egerton.

Harry Egerton.

Yes, probably they would.

Harvey Anderson.

That's just the point.

General Chadbourne.

Then who is responsible?

Harvey Anderson.

They'd gone to work.

Harry Egerton.

For this, I am. But for conditions here— —

General Chadbourne.

(*To Captain Haskell*)

Remember that.

Workmen.

No! We! We seized the mill!

Harry Egerton.

I led them.

Buck Bentley.

It was we unlocked the gates.

Workmen.

But we marched in, so we're responsible.

Harvey Anderson.

We won't dispute about who did it, partners.
There's glory enough for all.

(*Cheers*)

I'm in it too.

> (*He laughs*)

HARRY EGERTON.

> But for conditions that produced this strike
> God knows and I know it was not these men.
> I only wish that that was farther off.

GENERAL CHADBOURNE.

> If wrong's been done there's legal remedies.

HARRY EGERTON.

> Conditions, General, that outreach the law.

SAM WILLIAMS.

> For it's that 'open market' — —

VOICE.

> (*From the crowd*)

> Who makes the law?

SAM WILLIAMS.

> Their legal right to buy the cheapest men
> And drive them just as hard and just as long
> As they can stand it.

BUCK BENTLEY.

> And no troops are sent.

CRIES.

> (*Some militiamen joining in*)

> That's right!

WORKMEN.

> No troops for us! No troops for us!

> (*This cry is caught up by the crowd and is carried on back through the mill. Chadbourne looks at the militiamen and unbuttons his overcoat and feels about in his pockets*)

HARRY EGERTON.

> Pardon me, General, if I speak right out,
> But I've seen wages lowered to buy lands,
> And I've seen bread taken from these men here
> To gamble with. There are some things, General Chadbourne,

That can't go on. We've but one life to live
And we just can't stand by and see some things
And live. It's not worth while, it's not worth while.

BUCK BENTLEY.

And while you're here I want to say a word,
For possibly we won't see you any more,
And they'll be asking of us up the State.
I never thought of it — —

GENERAL CHADBOURNE.

(*Handing Haskell a notebook*)

Take down their names.

BUCK BENTLEY.

Till Mr. Egerton made his talk that day;
But it's a fact and it stares you in the face:
When Companies are wronged, or think they are,
They touch the wires and the troops are sent,
But when the men are wronged, or think they are,
It's 'legal remedies.'

SAM WILLIAMS.

That's well put, Comrade.

HARVEY ANDERSON.

That don't mean anything.

FIRST MILITIAMAN.

(*To Haskell*)

John Stamper.

FIRST GUARD.

I
Guess you know me.

SECOND MILITIAMAN.

And you can take mine, too.

HARVEY ANDERSON.

Who ever saw the like of this before!

THIRD MILITIAMAN.

Kelley.

SECOND GUARD.

> And mine.

HARRY EGERTON.

> A hundred years from now
> They'll write them in the larger book of Fame.

FOURTH MILITIAMAN.

> This is the third time we've been out this year.

HARVEY ANDERSON.

> You look like Israel Putnam and Paul Jones.

BUCK BENTLEY.

> We came down here to see the square thing done;
> But it's got to work both ways.

SIXTH MILITIAMAN.

> And mine.

SEVENTH MILITIAMAN.

> And mine.

HARVEY ANDERSON.

> *(To Chadbourne)*
>
> You're all right, partner, only you don't see
> The inside of this thing that's happened here.
> The day's gone by when two or three big men
> Could ride her to and fro for their own gain
> And lay her up and starve the crew. That's past.
> We're going to take the flags down of the Kings,
> Kings of Lumber, Kings of Cotton, Kings of Coal,
> From one end to the other of this land,
> And we'll all be Americans, North and South
> And East and West until you touch the seas.
> And there's the thing that's going to fly the mast.
>
> *(Points to the flag on the floor)*
>
> And when she climbs you'll hear the guns go off
> Announcing a new Independence here.
>
> *(Tremendous cheering)*

(Two militiamen are seen coming up the stairs, the one loaded with blankets, the other with ten or twelve rifles)

GENERAL CHADBOURNE.

(To Harry Egerton)

And this is final, eh?

VOICE.

(From the crowd)

We'll hold the mill!

WORKMEN.

(Catching sight of the two militiamen)

And the mine too! That's right! And the mine too!

(Tremendous cheering)

HARRY EGERTON.

If you have any way to guarantee
That these men who have worked here many years
And faithfully, as I know, will have their right
To work respected and at an honest wage,
And that while there are profits to be shared
There'll be no starving time among these men — —

GENERAL CHADBOURNE.

Don't think because you're Mr. Egerton
That you're immune. You'll find the laws the same
Whether you're Mr. Egerton or not.

(Starts for the stairs)

If need be I'll call out ten thousand men.

VOICE.

(Back in the mill)

Bring on the Constitution and let's vote!

FIFTH MILITIAMAN.

(With the paper)

You'll have your hands full if reports are true.

HARRY EGERTON.

We none of us can tell what men will do.
The times are changing and the days bring light.

GENERAL CHADBOURNE.

You mean you'll stir up mutiny again?

HARRY EGERTON.

I'll see they get the truth, then let them choose.
That is a right we all have, General Chadbourne.

GENERAL CHADBOURNE.

You'll have no chance to see them.

(Goes down the stairs, the two guards leading the way)

HARRY EGERTON.

Very well.
Just say to Governor Braddock it's with him.
We'll keep right on at work. The gates shall be
Open and the men shall come and go.

CAPTAIN HASKELL.

(To two militiamen who are busy stringing the flag on the rope)

Damn pretty men you are to raise a flag.
You ought to have a red one.

FIRST MILITIAMAN.

Go on, Haskell.

SECOND MILITIAMAN.

We'll see what kind of men dare take it down.

CAPTAIN HASKELL.

Wait till Court Martial sits.

*(Disappears down the stairs. There is a movement of the workmen back
into the mill)*

HARVEY ANDERSON.

(Shouting)

Now let's to work!

*(The militiamen gather left, and to some of them the rifles, knapsacks,
etc., are distributed. Buck Bentley, who has taken the bugles in his
hands, walks to and fro)*

HARVEY ANDERSON.

You'd better be off, Bentley, don't you think?
They'll turn Hell upside down to get that mine.

BUCK BENTLEY.

He wanted to say something to me.

Harvey Anderson.

> *(Calls rear left to Harry Egerton, who is engaged with Dicey, a number*
> *of workmen being gathered about them)*

Partner!

> *(They stand silent, watching the group)*

Buck Bentley.

Harry's too easy with him.

A Workman.

> *(Leaving the group and passing rear, calls to Anderson)*

The same old sore.

Harvey Anderson.

You've noticed any change these past few days?

Buck Bentley.

In Egerton, you mean? Ain't it the strain
Of breaking with his family?

> *(Harry Egerton starts toward them, but Dicey keeps after him, the men*
> *following)*

Buck Bentley.

> *(To Anderson, who has turned aside and half pulled from his inside*
> *pocket a legal looking document)*

What — —

Harvey Anderson.

His will.

Harry Egerton.

> *(To Dicey)*

It's a new day, my friend, a glorious day.

Voice.

> *(Back in the mill)*

'Twill soon be night!

Harry Egerton.

Try to forget the past
And everything except that we are men
Working together for the good of all.

Wes Dicey.

> That ain't the point though, Mr. Egerton.

Sam Williams.

> You've got your vote, Wes, same as we have ours,
> You and your friends have. Why ain't that enough?
> Or is it that you think the few should rule?

Wes Dicey.

> There's got to be good feelin' all around
> If it's to hold together as you say;
> It's got to be plumbed well. And I don't see,
> If it's to be a workers' commonwealth,
> How you can keep the mine out. Course it's yours
> And in a way you can do as you please,
> That is, if you was like most men you could;
> But bein' different, standin' for the right,
> We don't just see how you can say 'We'll keep
> The mine out and devote it to the Cause.'
> If the boys ain't the Cause, tell us what is.
> Maybe it's as we're ignorant and don't know.

Harry Egerton.

> Please do not put things in this bitter way.
> The Cause is what you've fought for all these years,
> A chance to live a freer, larger life.
> But in this struggle are you men alone?
> And shall we as we climb to better things
> Reach down no help to others, but hold fast
> To all we get?

Several.

> No! No!

Harry Egerton.

> Would that be right?

Wes Dicey.

> Another point. For years and years we've had
> A Union here, and when the fight came on,
> 'Twas as a Union that we made the fight.
> And Sam knows this is true, 'twas not so much
> The cut in wages, though, that took our strength,
> As 'twas their breakin' of the Union up
> As made us say 'By God, we'll fight or die.'

Ain't that true, boys?

TWO OR THREE.

That's true.

WES DICEY.

And then you come
And took the stand you did as they'd no right
To make slaves of us, closin' of the gates
To make us knuckle down. And you said 'Come,'
And the boys followed you, and here they are.
And many of 'em, if I sound 'em right,
Are wonderin' what we're here for. I'll ask Sam
If he's in favor of the Open Shop.

SAM WILLIAMS.

We formed our Union, Wes, when we were slaves,
Same as in war times armies are called out.
But when the war is over they go back.

WES DICEY.

'Go back.'

SAM WILLIAMS.

We're free men now.

CHRIS KNUDSON.

We've no foe now
Except ourselves.

WES DICEY.

All of which means you'll vote
In favor of admittin' every man
To full rights here.

HARVEY ANDERSON.

Look here, pard — —

WES DICEY.

Are you Sam?

HARVEY ANDERSON.

If it's the soldier boys you're knocking at,
They don't intend to stay, most of them don't.
But as I think they'll be invited to.

(*Cheers*)

Didn't they leave *their* Union?

A MILITIAMAN.

The damned dog.

SAM WILLIAMS.

I mean to vote, Wes, for that Living Mill
That Mr. Egerton has told us of.
For that's the thing, or something like that thing,
We've worked for all these years. And now it's come,
A place where we can work and be free men,
Having a say in things, as Harvey says,
God help us if we can't get on as friends.

(*Jim King takes Dicey aside, where Masters joins them*)

HARRY EGERTON.

(*Coming to Bentley and the militiamen*)

I want to thank you, Bentley, and you men,
I want to thank you for the help you've been.
You've played the noblest part I ever knew.

BUCK BENTLEY.

We followed you.

HARRY EGERTON.

No. We have interests here,
The rest of us have interests here; we've homes
And families, and the fight was ours. But you,
You'd never seen a one of us before.
And you came here honorable men, and now
You're traitors through the State, and mutineers.

BUCK BENTLEY.

It's all right.

HARRY EGERTON.

Yes, indeed, it is all right.

FIFTH MILITIAMAN.

They'll be more, too.

SIXTH MILITIAMAN.

He'll never call them out.

HARRY EGERTON.

> You've helped to make the history of this land,
> And there's not one of you will not be known
> And honored for it.

A MILITIAMAN.

> Half as much as you.

HARRY EGERTON.

> And now a little toast before you go.
>
> *(Shakes hands with them)*
>
> Bentley, Kelley, Stamper, and you all,
> Sam, and you, Harvey, Chris, and Mike, and Wes,
> You'll join us, you and Jim and Rome?
>
> *(The three remain aside talking together)*

HARRY EGERTON.

> And you,
> And you back there, you of the Living Mill—
> For all time, shall we say it?

SUBDUED VOICES.

> For all time.

HARRY EGERTON.

> *(With a swift glance toward Dicey, King and Masters)*
>
> And give our lives, if need be, for this thing?

SUBDUED VOICES.

> And give our lives, if need be, for this thing.

HARRY EGERTON.

> This is a glorious day.

MILITIAMEN.

> *(Leaving)*
>
> So long! So long!

HARRY EGERTON.

> Wherever men get free they'll think of us.

WORKMEN.

> So long! So long!

BUCK BENTLEY.

> And there was something else.
> The General came while you were speaking.

HARRY EGERTON.

> Ah!

BUCK BENTLEY.

> Something about some bugles you said get.

HARRY EGERTON.

> Yes, I forgot. I meant to show you these
> That a Committee brought this afternoon.
>
> *(Takes a paper from his pocket)*
>
> Read them in the meeting, Harvey.

CRIES.

> Read them now!

HARRY EGERTON.

> Some resolutions of the citizens,
> Who are glad we've gone on peaceably to work.
> And if at any time we need their help——

SAM WILLIAMS.

> *(Taking a bugle and holding it up to the crowd)*
>
> The citizens say blow these if we need help!
> Because we've gone on peaceably to work.
>
> *(Cheers)*
>
> It's work, you see, that wins, comrades.

CHRIS KNUDSON.

> That's right.

HARRY EGERTON.

> I trust, though, that they'll never need to blow.

BUCK BENTLEY.

> 'Twill set the land on fire if they do.

A WORKMAN.

> The workingmen throughout the State will hear.

HARVEY ANDERSON.

They'll blow in relay, pards, from sea to sea.

(*Harry Egerton stands and watches the militiamen depart. As Bentley goes down the stairs he turns and looks at Harry Egerton, who lifts his hand to his head in a sort of military salute*)

CHRIS KNUDSON.

That's what they say about us, Wes, you know
That when the thing we've fought is taken away
We'll fight among ourselves.

WES DICEY.

(*To Harry Egerton*)

I ain't a man,
And never have been one, to set my views
Against the boys' views. If they're satisfied
And think the new way's better than the old,
And if they'll vote for it, Wes and his friends
Will have no grouch.

SEVERAL.

That's all right.

A VOICE.

Then come on.

HARRY EGERTON.

To get along together, as Sam says,
That's what we seek, my friend. The rest will come.

WES DICEY.

It's for the boys I took the stand I did.

(*The workmen go back into the mill. Harry Egerton watches Dicey until he is lost among the men that pass out rear*)

HARVEY ANDERSON.

(*Who has been watching him*)

Partner.

HARRY EGERTON.

(*Who has started to follow the men*)

What is it, Harvey?

HARVEY ANDERSON.

What's this mean?

HARRY EGERTON.

> We cannot be too patient with these men.
> It's a free mill we're trying to build, Harvey.

HARVEY ANDERSON.

> 'Tain't that I mean.
>
> > (*Takes the will from his pocket*)
>
> Why did you give me this?

HARRY EGERTON.

> As a precaution, Harvey.

HARVEY ANDERSON.

> > (*To Jim King, who lingers about beyond the railing*)
>
> We'll be there.

HARRY EGERTON.

> If anything should happen to me, you know,
> My father would inherit everything.

HARVEY ANDERSON.

> Yes.

HARRY EGERTON.

> And God meant the mine for other things.
> And as administrators you and Sam
> And Buck I knew would carry on the work.

HARVEY ANDERSON.

> But why just now? Come on and tell me, partner.
> There's something up. You ain't been like yourself.
> There's something on your heart. What is it, partner?
> It ain't the faction?

HARRY EGERTON.

> No.

HARVEY ANDERSON.

> About the mine—
> That lie they told is eating in your heart.

HARRY EGERTON.

> Have I done anything that you know, Harvey,
> That could have wronged the men or any of them?

HARVEY ANDERSON.

You wronged them? What you mean?

HARRY EGERTON.

In any way?

HARVEY ANDERSON.

Why they'd die for you, partner. What you mean?

HARRY EGERTON.

Come here to-night when we can be alone.
There are some things I want to tell you, Harvey,
That you and Sam and Buck must carry out.

HARVEY ANDERSON.

(*Looks at him a long while, then lays his hands upon his shoulders*)

We're on the eve of seeing things come true
And there ain't nothing that can stop it, partner.

HARRY EGERTON.

I don't know what I'd do without you, Harvey.

(*They go back through the gate in the railing and out through the great door, left, whence the crowd has passed. Rome Masters comes furtively up the stairs and looks about. He then comes past the sash to the door, forward left, and begins to pull off the strip that is nailed across it. He has just loosened it when Jim King appears upon the stairs and gives a low whistle. Rome Masters quickly joins him and together they hurry back through the mill and out the great door, left. A moment later the First Guard comes up the stairs, followed by Ralph Ardsley and Bishop Hardbrooke*)

FIRST GUARD.

I'll find him.

BISHOP HARDBROOKE.

If you please.

(*The Guard goes back through the mill*)

BISHOP HARDBROOKE.

I don't like this.
The atmosphere's too charged with victory.

RALPH ARDSLEY.

I don't believe they even know it's cold.

(*Looks about*)

It's wonderful the way he's handled things.
It's that, I think, as much as anything
That's won the confidence of the citizens.
I was just sure they'd have a riot here.

(*He gets up on one of the stools before the desk and takes from his overcoat pocket a newspaper which he spreads out before him*)

I've thought about it, Bishop; don't you think
That that injunction Egerton got out
Against the mine, considering everything,
The public feeling—if he has good grounds
For claiming that his own men found the mine—
Aside from the reflection on his son—
A tactical mistake, don't you think so?

BISHOP HARDBROOKE.

Best not allude to that.

RALPH ARDSLEY.

I think so too.

(*He reads the paper. The Bishop stands listening to the indistinct noises
that come from the crowd outside*)

RALPH ARDSLEY.

And yet you can't blame Jergens very much.
Something has got to happen pretty soon.
Amalgamated's off again, I see.

BISHOP HARDBROOKE.

Who is this Harvey Anderson?

RALPH ARDSLEY.

He's the rough
That kept the men from going back that day.
Drew his revolver. Big man here now. You see
He'd been out on the mountains with a cast,
One of the men the Company had out.
So it's quite possible, as Jergens claims,
That Anderson found the mine. For gold these days—
To get possession of a mine like that—
Men have been killed for less.

BISHOP HARDBROOKE.

But Harry——

RALPH ARDSLEY.

> That,
> That's what I can't get down me, his collusion — —

> > (*Cheers outside*)

> It's probably Anderson haranguing them.
> I don't myself believe that Harry'd do it.

> > > (*Tremendous cheering*)

> There's certainly enthusiasm there.

BISHOP HARDBROOKE.

> What is it, Editor Ardsley?

RALPH ARDSLEY.

> I don't know.

BISHOP HARDBROOKE.

> What's it all mean? What's underneath it all?

RALPH ARDSLEY.

> We're neither of us, Bishop, what we were.
> We've lost our power. Something's happening
> That we don't understand.

> > (*A pause*)

> And done by men
> That live right here and walk the streets and talk,
> Buy vegetables and pass the time of day.
> I tell you, Bishop Hardbrooke, you can't tell.

BISHOP HARDBROOKE.

> > (*Half to himself*)

> As though they had the Ark of the Covenant.

RALPH ARDSLEY.

> If any one had said to me last week
> That that despondent crowd of shabby men,
> After six weeks of battle against odds,
> And beaten into silence, starved and cold,
> Had in them the capacity for this —
> Who was it said we're always in a flux,
> That nothing's fixed? We don't know anything.
> It's like a case of type; to-day it spells
> Egerton and to-morrow M-o-b.
> To think of Donald Egerton at bay!

Egad!

BISHOP HARDBROOKE.

These shouts once rose about the Church,
But somehow we don't hear them any more.

RALPH ARDSLEY.

Don't think for a moment, Bishop, that you're alone.
We never had the tumult and the shout
That you had in old days, but it's all the same.
The 'Power of the Press'! It makes me laugh.
If I could find a little farm somewhere,
I'd sell my stock to Egerton and get out
And let the world go hang. I'm tired of it.

> *(Cheers outside)*

Yes, there's a ring about it you don't hear
Even in Conventions.

(The Guard enters the mill, back left, and comes through the gate in the railing)

GUARD.

In a moment.

BISHOP HARDBROOKE.

Thank you.

> *(The Guard goes out down the stairs)*

RALPH ARDSLEY.

What's your opinion of the trouble, Bishop?

> *(To himself)*

To think of Donald Egerton at bay!

BISHOP HARDBROOKE.

We've had the matter up in Conference
Several times.

RALPH ARDSLEY.

Yes.

BISHOP HARDBROOKE.

But I somehow feel
We don't get hold of it. The lower classes—
They're going off. I don't believe it's Christ.

You say they're leaving you; and General Chadbourne—
Two thirds, I think you said, of his command.

RALPH ARDSLEY.

Facing State's prison, too

> (*Cheers outside. The two men remain silent*)

RALPH ARDSLEY.

And Egerton—
They certainly have left him. I thought last night
As I sat looking up toward that new home—

> (*Cheers outside*)

They'll never light it up again that way,
The way it was that day. Did you ever see
Anything to equal that reception hall?

BISHOP HARDBROOKE.

What's in the boy that these men follow him,
And all his life so quiet, almost timid?

RALPH ARDSLEY.

'What go ye out into the wilderness for to see?'

BISHOP HARDBROOKE.

Yes, if his cause were better.

RALPH ARDSLEY.

There you are.

BISHOP HARDBROOKE.

But this audacious, this deliberate
Stealing—though I hate to use the word—
This seizing of the mill——

RALPH ARDSLEY.

Here he comes now.

> (*He gets down from the stool*)

You do the talking, Bishop, the heavy part.

> (*Harry Egerton enters*)

BISHOP HARDBROOKE.

Harry.

HARRY EGERTON.

Bishop Hardbrooke.

RALPH ARDSLEY.

You don't seem
To mind the cold or anything down here.

HARRY EGERTON.

We have been busy.

RALPH ARDSLEY.

I should think so. Yes
It's wonderful the way you've plunged right in
To business.

HARRY EGERTON.

Yes.

RALPH ARDSLEY.

Things going pretty well?

HARRY EGERTON.

Yes.

RALPH ARDSLEY.

I'm glad.

HARRY EGERTON.

You sent for me.

RALPH ARDSLEY.

Yes.

BISHOP HARDBROOKE.

Harry,
We've come to see if something can't be done
To end this controversy and bring peace,
An honorable peace to all concerned.
A permanent state of strife is far from pleasant.
There's nothing sadder in the life of man
Than to see towns disrupted, classes arrayed
Against each other, to say nothing, Harry,
Of this far dearer tie that's straining here,
That pains us all far more than we can tell.
We've often had these troubles in the Church,
Mostly in the past, of course, men differing

Upon some point of doctrine or government.
And my experience is that at the bottom
There's something that at first was overlooked,
Then, in the strife that followed, overwhelmed.
There's common ground, there must be in these things.
Look at the world; we pass along the street.
We don't confront each other and block the way.
Each yields a bit and so we all pass on.
And in relationships it must be the same.
We're one, my brother.

RALPH ARDSLEY.

Like our fingers here.

BISHOP HARDBROOKE.

And when we're not, when interests seem to clash,
It's just as sure as Death or anything
Some law of God is being tampered with.
And so we thought we'd come— —

RALPH ARDSLEY.

And now's the time.

BISHOP HARDBROOKE.

For, as you know, in town the feeling's growing
That there's a sword impending over us
Which the least breath will bring down on our heads.

RALPH ARDSLEY.

And not in the town alone, but the whole State—
They seem to have their eyes upon us here.
You've seen the papers how the strikes are spreading.
The mills at Upton and the plant at Sawyer,
And down the State there's Smith and Balding Brothers,
Heacox and Knight, twelve hundred men gone out,
Demanding unconditionally the mills.

BISHOP HARDBROOKE.

Think of it, Harry, think of what this means!

RALPH ARDSLEY.

Not satisfied with wages any more.

HARRY EGERTON.

Pardon me.

(*Walks rear and listens*)

BISHOP HARDBROOKE.

He doesn't listen to what I say.

RALPH ARDSLEY.

Not that you are to blame for it, we don't say that.
But probably without your knowing it
A fire or something's going out of you
That's kindling this industrial upheaval;
For it's your name they've made the war-cry, Harry.

BISHOP HARDBROOKE.

He even smiled when you spoke of the mills
Closing.

RALPH ARDSLEY.

I don't think he meant it so.
His heart's out there, though, that's as plain as day.

BISHOP HARDBROOKE.

Harry, if these shouts mean a final step,
A closing up of things which if once closed
Will render of no use any labor of ours,
I beg of you to call this meeting off,
At least until we see what we can do.

RALPH ARDSLEY.

Postpone it, Harry, say till Monday morning.
You know yourself how dangerous it is
To wake men's hopes to a wild dream of power.
They're never afterwards content with less
Than that wild something that could never be.

BISHOP HARDBROOKE.

Yes, brother, let the Lord's day with its peace
Breathe on this quarrel. Why do you say too late?

HARRY EGERTON.

(*Who has come forward*)

Because it's up there, Bishop, it's up there
Above mere bread.

RALPH ARDSLEY.

What does he mean by that?

BISHOP HARDBROOKE.

> I trust, my brother, that it is up there.

RALPH ARDSLEY.

> We don't just see what it is you are trying to do.

HARRY EGERTON.

> The statement I gave out last Saturday— —

RALPH ARDSLEY.

> That was a week ago.

HARRY EGERTON.

> Yes.

RALPH ARDSLEY.

> And since then
> Reports have come out that there's a move on foot
> To organize—I know not what to call it— —

HARRY EGERTON.

> A Commonwealth of Workers.

BISHOP HARDBROOKE.

> Then it's true!

RALPH ARDSLEY.

> Your purpose then is to retain the mill?

BISHOP HARDBROOKE.

> Purchase it?

HARRY EGERTON.

> I don't know. We'll do what's fair.
> We've had to think first of supplying bread.
> That's left but little time for other things.

BISHOP HARDBROOKE.

> But if the Company shouldn't choose to sell?

HARRY EGERTON.

> That is with them.

RALPH ARDSLEY.

> You mean you'll still hold on?

HARRY EGERTON.

That will be my advice, yes.

RALPH ARDSLEY.

But the Law.

BISHOP HARDBROOKE.

'Thou shalt not steal.'

(*Harry Egerton walks rear and listens*)

RALPH ARDSLEY.

Doesn't that beat the world!

BISHOP HARDBROOKE.

It's his association with these roughs.

RALPH ARDSLEY.

And they'll never dare lay hands upon them, Bishop.
I tell you the Commonwealth's afraid to move.

BISHOP HARDBROOKE.

Has God no place in business, my young brother?

HARRY EGERTON.

(*Returning*)

Yes, Bishop Hardbrooke, and it's very strange
You've never thought of that until to-day.

BISHOP HARDBROOKE.

A hidden meaning couched in that, I think.

HARRY EGERTON.

This is the first time you've been in this mill
Or near these workingmen in all these years.
And now you come to plead my father's cause.

BISHOP HARDBROOKE.

I come for peace.

HARRY EGERTON.

Then why not weeks ago
When there was strife? You heard the cry of the poor
For six weeks, Bishop, and you never came.
Why wait until the starving time is past?

Bishop Hardbrooke.

> I've rather arduous duties, my young brother.
> Besides my Church work there are Boards and Boards
> And meetings of this Charity and that
> That you in business know but little of.
> My interest in the poor is not unknown.

Harry Egerton.

> You've been in father's confidence for years.

Bishop Hardbrooke.

> I'm proud to say I have.

Harry Egerton.

> There's seldom passed
> A Sunday that he's not been in his pew.

Bishop Hardbrooke.

> A creditable record.

Ralph Ardsley.

> I should say.

Bishop Hardbrooke.

> And one that any son might emulate
> With profit, I should think.

Harry Egerton.

> It's very strange
> My father doesn't know some things are wrong.

Bishop Hardbrooke.

> You mean he doesn't see things as you do.

Harry Egerton.

> Yes, all my life I've wondered when I've seen
> Check after check go out with father's name
> To help along some Mission over sea
> Or roof some rising Charity at home,
> I've often wondered that he's never seen
> Those little shacks upon the hill out there
> Nor heard the cry of widows from these saws.

Bishop Hardbrooke.

> I would suggest, my brother, that we leave

The deeper things of God for quiet times
And turn our minds to something nearer home.

HARRY EGERTON.

I know of nothing nearer home than this,
The cry of men for justice at our doors.

BISHOP HARDBROOKE.

Suppose we get the Company to agree
To let bygones be bygones with the men,
And to restore conditions as they were— —

RALPH ARDSLEY.

In other words to meet the men's demands.

BISHOP HARDBROOKE.

And put the guards they ask about the saws.
That would remove the causes, would it not,
Of the misunderstanding?

RALPH ARDSLEY.

Every one.

BISHOP HARDBROOKE.

Would there be any valid reason then
Why Peace should not return and all be friends
As formerly?

HARRY EGERTON.

For weeks they waited for it.

(Listens back)

BISHOP HARDBROOKE.

What's time to do with right and wrong, my brother?

HARRY EGERTON.

But men in misery often have a vision
Beyond the eye of prosperous days to see.

BISHOP HARDBROOKE.

If it was fair last week, then why not now?

HARRY EGERTON.

They're building something fairer.

(Walks back)

RALPH ARDSLEY.

It's no use.

BISHOP HARDBROOKE.

On what foundations, Harry? All about
I see the wreck and ruin of our land;
Her altars down, her sacred institutions— —

(*Cheering outside*)

Harry, I beg of you to stop and think
What it has cost, this Law that you defy
And cast before the swine of riotous feet.

(*Continuous cheering*)

I appeal to you, my brother— —

HARRY EGERTON.

Bishop Hardbrooke— —

BISHOP HARDBROOKE.

In the name of everything that you hold dear— —

HARRY EGERTON.

There's nothing you could say that could persuade me— —

BISHOP HARDBROOKE.

Think of your country plunged in civil war!

HARRY EGERTON.

To stay even with a word what's rising there.

BISHOP HARDBROOKE.

Think of your mother, think of how she feels
Sitting— —

RALPH ARDSLEY.

Here's Anderson!

HARRY EGERTON.

What is it, Harvey?

HARVEY ANDERSON.

(*Hurrying in*)

Well, President of Free Mill Number One
And many more hereafter!

(*Goes quickly left and, seizing the rope, pulls the flag up on the pole*)

Up the mast,
My beauty! Now you'll hear 'em raise the roof.

HARRY EGERTON.

And Dicey——?

HARVEY ANDERSON.

Moved to make it unanimous.
No opposition.

(*Tremendous cheering outside*)

HARVEY ANDERSON.

(*Comes right and takes Harry Egerton's two hands in his*)

Well, boy?

RALPH ARDSLEY.

It's no use, Bishop.

HARVEY ANDERSON.

You've dreamed it and it's a fact now, partner.

HARRY EGERTON.

Yes.

HARVEY ANDERSON.

The years will multiply 'em.

HARRY EGERTON.

Hear! Just hear!

(*Prolonged cheering*)

RALPH ARDSLEY.

Let's leave 'em and let 'em stew in their own juice.

HARRY EGERTON.

The Living Mill!

(*A volley of shots*)

HARVEY ANDERSON.

There goes the boys' salute!

(*Seizes Harry Egerton by the shoulders and lifts him off his feet*)

Up with you, up into the skies with you!

We've lived to see a day will live forever.
And you come right on out and make your speech.

> (*Hurries back through the mill*)

HARRY EGERTON.

I'll be there shortly, Harvey.

BISHOP HARDBROOKE.

I suppose
There's no use in our talking any more.

HARRY EGERTON.

I'm sorry, Bishop.

BISHOP HARDBROOKE.

Then — Good-bye.

HARRY EGERTON.

Good-bye.

> (*The Bishop and Ardsley go out down the stairs. Harry Egerton starts
> back toward the gate*)

JIM KING.

> (*Suddenly appears just beyond the railing*)

There was a call just now 'fore you came in.
I think it was your mother.

> (*Harry Egerton turns back to the desk and takes up the telephone. Jim
> King vanishes through the great door, left*)

HARRY EGERTON.

Forty-nine
Grand View, please. Yes.

> (*A pause*)

Mother? I knew your voice.
You called me up, one of the men said. No?

> (*A pause*)

Or some one else.

> (*A pause*)

Yes, mother, very well.
You're going to the city?

> (*A pause*)

That was it.
I thought perhaps you had called me up to ask.

> (*A pause*)

Four or five hundred pounds.

> (*A pause*)

Mixed, I should say.
And such toys as you think children would like.

> (*A pause*)

O you know more about such things than I.

> (*A pause*)

Yes.

> (*A pause*)

Mother, while I think of it, has father
Had any trouble with Jergens?

> (*A pause*)

Ah, I'm glad.
I overheard him talking with some men
The other night, and thought from what he said
It might be father they were talking of.

> (*A pause. The door, forward left, opens slowly and Rome Masters
> comes stealthily in with a bar of iron in his hand, and moves toward
> Harry Egerton, whose back is to him*)

Harry Egerton.

I'm very glad. You might ask father though.

> (*Cheering outside*)

I'll have some news for you when you return.

> (*A pause*)

Here in the mill. And I'll be Santa Claus.

> (*A pause*)

That will be beautiful.

> (*A pause*)

And, mother— —

> (*Masters strikes him*)

Harry Egerton.

Ah!

(*He sinks to the floor. Masters, iron in hand, flees down the stairs. The cheering outside continues. Then, as the noise subsides, there is heard a steady buzzing of the telephone as though some one were trying to get connection)*

ACT V

CHRISTMAS EVE

Scene: Inside the large room of a newly built board cabin up at the mine. Centre, rear, the open mouth of the tunnel, with the wall resting upon the rocks above. Left, in this same wall, near the corner, a door opening outside. Right, near the other corner, about four feet up from the floor, a small oblong window through which one sees the snow lying thick upon the mountains, and beyond the snow the dark of the sky with the winter stars shining brightly. In the right wall, well back, a door opens into a bedroom. Centre, in the opposite wall, a second door opens into a sort of woodshed. Left, a little way to the rear from the centre of the room, a heavy iron stove with chairs standing about. A woodbox is over near the wall, left. Forward right, a table with a bugle lying upon two or three sheets of loose paper, and, farther over, a heap of ore samples in which, with the light of the near-by lamp falling upon them, the gold is plainly visible.

Harvey Anderson, his hat pulled low over his eyes, sits with his back to the bedroom, staring at the stove. The only motion discernible is an occasional pressing of the lip when he bites his moustache. Later, Mrs. Egerton, careworn and evidently in deep distress, enters from the bedroom and starts to say something to Harvey Anderson, but decides not to. Instead she goes to the window and stands looking out as though she were anxiously waiting for some one.

Time: Christmas Eve.

MRS. EGERTON.

> *(In a low voice)*

It's after midnight, for the lights are out
Down in the town. It must be after one.

> *(Speaks back as though into the bedroom)*

You think the guard would let him come right through?

HARVEY ANDERSON.

Yes, mother.

MRS. EGERTON.

I didn't mean to wake you, Harvey.

HARVEY ANDERSON.

I ain't been sleeping.

MRS. EGERTON.

But it seems so long.

(*Turns again to the window*)

HARVEY ANDERSON.

The snow's so deep upon the mountains, mother.
And Sam and Chris—I know they'd hurry on—
They ain't come either.

NURSE.

(*Entering from the bedroom*)

It's stopped snowing now.

HARVEY ANDERSON.

It's getting colder. How's he seem to be?

NURSE.

There's very little change. What time is it?

HARVEY ANDERSON.

(*Looks at his watch*)

Going on half past three.

(*They look at one another*)

NURSE.

Don't think such things.

(*Anderson goes to the woodbox and looks in*)

MRS. EGERTON.

(*At the window, to herself*)

If I only knew! If I only knew he'd come!

NURSE.

(*As Anderson goes into the woodshed*)

He may have telegraphed for specialists.

(*She glances toward Mrs. Egerton, then goes quietly to the door, rear
left, and looks out*)

NURSE.

(*Comes back*)

I wish that there was something that I could do.

MRS. EGERTON.

You made it plain that he must come at once?

NURSE.

Yes, Mrs. Egerton. I told the truth.
Some think it's better to deceive. I don't.
And I find that people thank you in the end.

MRS. EGERTON.

And they've been gone since nine.

NURSE.

Lie down a while,
Won't you? I wish you would.

MRS. EGERTON.

Isn't that some one?

NURSE.

(Goes to the window)

It's Mr. Bentley with the guard, I think.

(Mrs. Egerton leaves the window and walks about the room)

MRS. EGERTON.

(Half to herself)

The stars are so low down, so beautiful;
And the world so full of joy. Isn't it strange?
To-day we're here and to-morrow somewheres else.

(She stops by the bedroom door and stands looking in)

NURSE.

He's so your boy.

MRS. EGERTON.

Yes, yes.

NURSE.

And he loves you so.
It's always 'mother' when he speaks at all;
You and the mill.

(A pause)

And then you'll always know
There's never been a man in Foreston
Been loved as he has been.

MRS. EGERTON.

But he's so young!
And his work—He'd just begun. So little chance!

NURSE.

I've nursed so many cases of old men,
And men in prosperous circumstances, too,
Who've had no friends at all, just relatives.

> (*Mrs. Egerton walks about*)

NURSE.

And friends are so much closer, don't you think?

MRS. EGERTON.

Has he never, never mentioned Donald's name
In his delirium?

NURSE.

> (*Shakes her head*)

But then you know
Those first weeks at the Hospital were a blank,
Or almost so. And then when he came to
After the operation— —

MRS. EGERTON.

Donald! Donald!

NURSE.

I being a stranger, just a nurse, you know.
In delirium of course it's different.
But then I'd left the case.

> (*Harvey Anderson enters with an armful of wood*)

NURSE.

I was surprised
When I got word from Mr. Anderson
That you had let him—It's so far up here.

MRS. EGERTON.

He wanted to so much.

NURSE.

> They always do.
> But they don't always know what's best for them.

HARVEY ANDERSON.

> But he was getting on so well.

NURSE.

> I know.

HARVEY ANDERSON.

> There was no fever till four days ago.

NURSE.

> *(To Mrs. Egerton)*
>
> When I got here he was quite rational.

HARVEY ANDERSON.

> And talked about the mine here and the mill.
> And figured out the timber that we'd need
> For next year's run. I don't know what it was.
>
> *(Quietly replenishes the fire)*

MRS. EGERTON.

> *(At the bedroom door)*
>
> He hasn't moved.

NURSE.

> It quite exhausted him.

MRS. EGERTON.

> You think he recognized me?

NURSE.

> I don't know.

HARVEY ANDERSON.

> *(Who has come to the table, picks up one of the sheets of paper)*
>
> And he was planning homes here for the men
> Upon the valley land, with flowers and trees.

NURSE.

> Wasn't it strange that he should hear the bells?

HARVEY ANDERSON.

I hadn't heard them till he spoke.

NURSE.

Nor I.

HARVEY ANDERSON.

He seemed to know that it is Christmas Eve.

MRS. EGERTON.

His speaking of the toys!

NURSE.

Lie down a while.

HARVEY ANDERSON.

It's all right, mother, it's all right.

NURSE.

Won't you?
We'll call you when he comes.

BUCK BENTLEY.

(*Entering hurriedly from outside*)

Here comes a light.

MRS. EGERTON.

(*Collecting herself*)

If there's anything, Harvey, anything I can do
To help the work along, you'll come to me.
Promise me that. And you must keep right on.

HARVEY ANDERSON.

Yes, mother. We talked of that.

(*Mrs. Egerton kisses him and goes into the bedroom*)

BUCK BENTLEY.

How is he now?

NURSE.

About the same.

(*She goes to the window*)

BUCK BENTLEY.

You didn't think he'd come.

HARVEY ANDERSON.

He's been six weeks, almost. But that's all right.
Is the Doctor with him?

BUCK BENTLEY.

Yes.

> (*Starts for the door*)

I'll tell the boys.

HARVEY ANDERSON.

Then come back, Buck.

BUCK BENTLEY.

I will.

> (*He goes out. Anderson stands staring at the door*)

NURSE.

I'm so, so glad.
These weeks and weeks— —It's been so hard to bear.
You see when Death comes, Mr. Anderson—
It ought to be a lesson to us all.
You'll stay, of course.

HARVEY ANDERSON.

I? Sure.

NURSE.

He's felt so hard,
So bitter toward you.

> (*Buck Bentley enters quickly. Looks from Harvey to the Nurse*)

HARVEY ANDERSON.

What?— —

BUCK BENTLEY.

It's Sam and Chris.

> (*Sam Williams and Chris Knudson come in with a lantern*)

HARVEY ANDERSON.

See anything of Egerton coming up?

> (*The men show surprise*)

Buck Bentley.

They sent for him.

Sam Williams.

Is he as bad as that?

Harvey Anderson.

He hasn't been himself.

(To Bentley, who starts out)

Then come back.

Buck Bentley.

Yes.

(Anderson turns and shakes his head at the Nurse, who goes into the
bedroom, closing the door after her)

Harvey Anderson.

He spoke of both of you.

Chris Knudson.

Too bad! too bad!

Harvey Anderson.

I thought you'd like to be here.

(They sit silent about the stove)

Harvey Anderson.

Colder.

Chris Knudson.

Yes.

(They are silent)

Harvey Anderson.

Things going all right, Sam?

(Sam Williams nods)

Harvey Anderson.

And in the camps?

Chris Knudson.

Hundred and fifty men.

(They are silent)

Sam Williams.

> There's a report
> That Masters will turn State's evidence.

Harvey Anderson.

> Good news.

Chris Knudson.

> The citizens are pressing on the case.

Harvey Anderson.

> They'll find the trail leads where we said.

Chris Knudson.

> That's sure.

Sam Williams.

> His throwing down the silver don't help though.
>
> *(They are silent)*

Harvey Anderson.

> You see about those young pines, Chris. With spring
> We'll begin setting out as partner wished,
> And start all over with the land all green.
>
> *(They are silent)*

Chris Knudson.

> The boys will be so sorry.

Harvey Anderson.

> I don't mind,
> Now that it can't be, telling you of a plan— —
>
> *(There is a slight noise in the bedroom. Anderson turns and listens; but everything becomes quiet again)*

Harvey Anderson.

> Of a surprise he had for Christmas day,
> For all of us and the families of the men.

Nurse.

> *(Appears at the door and calls quickly)*
>
> Harvey!

(Anderson starts for the bedroom. Suddenly Harry Egerton appears

*struggling with his mother and the Nurse. His head is bandaged and
his face is covered with a six weeks' beard)*

HARRY EGERTON.

No, no! See there! see there! see there!
They're here already!

*(A shadowy line of workmen with their wives and children in their
Sunday clothes comes in left)*

HARRY EGERTON.

(Shouting right)

In the dry-kiln, Sam!
And fetch the other barrel, Harvey.

MRS. EGERTON.

Harry!

HARRY EGERTON.

A Merry Christmas, friends, to all of you!
I'm glad you've come!

(Shaking himself free)

It's all right, it's all right!
Candy, candy, candy, children!

(The children crowd about him)

MRS. EGERTON.

Harry!

HARRY EGERTON.

Let them come! let them come! There! there! there!

HARVEY ANDERSON.

Partner!

HARRY EGERTON.

(Laughing)

Isn't it wonderful!

MRS. EGERTON.

It's mother, Harry!

HARRY EGERTON.

And here's a little doll and here's a sled!

I brought them down over the chimney tops!

(*Laughs. A little boy remains after the other children have gone back to their parents*)

HARRY EGERTON.

A little horn?

HARVEY ANDERSON.

Partner!

HARRY EGERTON.

What golden hair!

(*The little boy returns to the others*)

HARRY EGERTON.

(*Advancing and shaking hands with the men and women, who file by him and pass out rear*)

Next year, my friends, if everything goes well,
We'll have some homes to hang up on the tree
With big yards where the little ones can play.
But this is children's day.

(*Last in the line comes a figure in the garb of a workman, but with the tender, bearded face of the Christ*)

HARRY EGERTON.

(*Looking at his brow*)

Have you been hurt?

(*The figure holds out both hands to him*)

HARRY EGERTON.

(*At first wildly, but with growing calmness*)

Harvey! Buck! Mother!

(*The figure looks back one moment, then vanishes. Harry Egerton is seen falling into the arms of Harvey Anderson, who carries him into the bedroom. His mother and the Nurse follow. Sam Williams and Chris Knudson stand staring across at the door*)

SAM WILLIAMS.

Our leader's gone, Chris.

CHRIS KNUDSON.

Yes, I fear so.

HARVEY ANDERSON.

> *(Coming in and closing the bedroom door after him)*

Partner's gone.

A GUARD.

> *(Pushing open the outside door)*

Egerton's come.

> *(Donald Egerton enters, followed by the Doctor and two strange men, apparently surgeons, one of them carrying an instrument case. Egerton glances about and instinctively locates the bedroom, and at once goes toward it)*

HARVEY ANDERSON.

> *(To the Doctor)*

Too late.

DOCTOR.

Dead!

HARVEY ANDERSON.

Just this moment.

VOICE OF MRS. EGERTON.

> *(As Egerton opens the bedroom door)*

Donald! Donald!

> *(The Doctor follows Egerton into the bedroom)*

CHRIS KNUDSON.

> *(Looking toward the door that the Doctor has shut)*

Peace and good will on earth.

HARVEY ANDERSON.

He stood for that.

> *(They stand silent about the stove. Anderson picks up two chairs, which he takes over to the two strangers, who are standing by the table)*

CHRIS KNUDSON.

There's things about us here that we don't see.

SAM WILLIAMS.

> *(Looking toward the bedroom)*

I'm sorry—for his sake.

CHRIS KNUDSON.

> What will we do?

SAM WILLIAMS.

> You'll not desert us, comrade, now he's gone.

HARVEY ANDERSON.

> 'For all time; shall we say it?'

CHRIS KNUDSON.

> That last day.

HARVEY ANDERSON.

> 'And give our lives, if need be?'

SAM WILLIAMS.

> He gave his.

> *(Takes up the lantern)*

HARVEY ANDERSON.

> He hasn't left the Cause, Sam.

SAM WILLIAMS.

> True.

CHRIS KNUDSON.

> That's true;
> He hasn't left the Cause.

HARVEY ANDERSON.

> Here just last week,
> Sitting about the table, planning things,
> 'The Cause will be here, Harvey, when we're gone,
> A beautiful river flowing through the land.'

CHRIS KNUDSON.

> There was the noblest boy this land's brought forth.

HARVEY ANDERSON.

> And we must make it wider, Sam.

SAM WILLIAMS.

> Yes, yes.

HARVEY ANDERSON.

Till the whole land is free. That's our work now.

Sam Williams.

Yes, we must keep right on.

Harvey Anderson.

That was his wish,
That we should keep right on; and his mother's, too.
Tell the boys that.

Sam Williams.

We will.

Chris Knudson.

There ought to be
A public funeral so the men could march.

Harvey Anderson.

I'll speak to Mr. Egerton.

First Stranger.

(Indicating Anderson)

That's him.

(The two workmen go out)

Harvey Anderson.

Stop by the cabins and tell Buck. Good-night.

*(He shuts the door and walks about, stopping occasionally by the stove,
absorbed in thought)*

Second Stranger.

He'll hardly use us now.

First Stranger.

Probably not.

(They take up pieces of the ore)

First Stranger.

(To Anderson, who is walking about)

How much does this assay?

Second Stranger.

He didn't hear you.

EGERTON.

        (Enters with the Doctor and speaks with him aside)

Drive down a mile or so and wait for me.

    (Mrs. Egerton and the Nurse come in. Both are dressed for travelling)

MRS. EGERTON.

        (Walks toward the outer door, then suddenly turns)

O Donald, Donald, this is Christmas Eve!
Think of this night in years gone by!

EGERTON.

        (Tenderly)

Mary!

NURSE.

'Thy will be done.'

HARVEY ANDERSON.

It's all right, mother.

MRS. EGERTON.

Harvey!

      (She embraces him and goes out with the Nurse)

EGERTON.

        (To the Doctor)

And you'll attend to everything?

DOCTOR.

Yes, Colonel.

(The Doctor goes out. Egerton shuts the door and stands for a moment apparently waiting till those who have just left get farther from the cabin. He then starts pacing to and fro as though he were undecided what to do. As he walks left toward Harvey Anderson his brow darkens. But as he turns right and draws near the bedroom the hard lines of his face relax. It is clear that a terrible struggle is going on within him)

EGERTON.

        (To Harvey Anderson)

You here alone?

HARVEY ANDERSON.

Yes, Mr. Egerton.
But that don't matter if there's anything— —

> (*Egerton stands for a moment, then resumes his walk*)

HARVEY ANDERSON.

Is there something I can do?

EGERTON.

> (*Stopping midway between the bedroom and Anderson, to the strang-*
> *ers*)

What do you say?

FIRST STRANGER.

We'll do the best we can.

> (*The Second Stranger removes his overcoat. The First lifts the instru-*
> *ment case upon the table and begins to open it. Egerton walks toward*
> *the bedroom*)

HARVEY ANDERSON.

> (*Following him*)

I don't believe—
I don't believe, though, Mr. Egerton,
It's any use.

FIRST STRANGER.

> (*Suddenly covering Anderson with pistols which he has taken from the*
> *case*)

Keep those hands where they are.
Bolt that door, Ned.

> (*The Second Detective bolts the outside door. He then comes to the table*
> *and takes from the case two pairs of handcuffs, a long black mackintosh,*
> *and a black cap*)

FIRST DETECTIVE.

Search him.

SECOND DETECTIVE.

> (*Feels about Anderson's hips and sides*)

Slip on this coat.

HARVEY ANDERSON.

> (*To Egerton, while the detective puts the coat on him*)

Well, partner, I've seen men where Hell was loud

Shoot from behind dead bodies but, by God,
I've never seen them shoot from such as him.

> (*Nodding toward the bedroom*)

FIRST DETECTIVE.

Quick now.

EGERTON.

You know the way?

HARVEY ANDERSON.

You beat them all.

FIRST DETECTIVE.

We keep the road to the left.

EGERTON.

Over the mountains.
You'll probably have some trouble.

FIRST DETECTIVE.

We'll get there.

EGERTON.

I'll have the Express wait for you at Lucasville.
You ought to reach there— —

> (*Looks at his watch*)

It's now five o'clock— —
By ten or eleven.

FIRST DETECTIVE.

At the outside.

(*The Second Detective hands to Egerton his son's will, which, in buttoning the coat up about Anderson, he has found in the latter's pocket*)

EGERTON.

> (*Looks into it a moment*)

Um!

SECOND DETECTIVE.

The guard will be off duty?

FIRST DETECTIVE.

I think so,

But we've no time to lose.

(*The Second Detective handcuffs himself to Anderson on the left side. The First Detective puts the cap on Anderson so that with the high collar of the coat turned up, only his eyes are visible under the poke*)

HARVEY ANDERSON.

The black cap, eh?

(*The First Detective then handcuffs himself to Anderson on the right side*)

EGERTON.

You wire me when you reach the Capitol.

FIRST DETECTIVE.

Yes, Mr. Egerton.

EGERTON.

Go briskly now.

FIRST DETECTIVE.

(*Showing Anderson his pistol*)

Now not a word from you, you understand.

(*He puts the pistol in his side overcoat pocket and keeps his hand on it*)

EGERTON.

'Twill soon be morning.

HARVEY ANDERSON.

Yes, you'd better leave
Before the land wakes up.

(*The detectives, with Anderson between them, go out*)

EGERTON.

We'll see, my man—

(*Puts the key on the outside of the door*)

How you'll shake down the pillars of this land.

(*He goes out and locks the door after him. A few moments pass. Suddenly at some distance outside a shot is heard. Again a few moments pass. Then, with a crash, the door is broken in and Buck Bentley, with the will in his hand, pulls himself hurriedly through the hole. He staggers to the table and seizes the bugle and blows a loud blast, then reels and, trying to steady himself, falls dead upon the floor, taking the table down with him. There is a clattering of the ore samples and a breaking of glass, and the lamp goes out, leaving the room in darkness. A half mile or so away, in the direction of Foreston, a bugle is heard, then, farther away, another, and fainter, another, and still another. And out through the window in the starlight of the Christmas morning soldiers with rifles in their hands are seen running rear left through the snow)*

Lector House believes that a society develops through a two-fold approach of continuous learning and adaptation, which is derived from the study of classic literary works spread across the historic timeline of literature records. Therefore, we aim at reviving, repairing and redeveloping all those inaccessible or damaged but historically as well as culturally important literature across subjects so that the future generations may have an opportunity to study and learn from past works to embark upon a journey of creating a better future.

This book is a result of an effort made by Lector House towards making a contribution to the preservation and repair of original ancient works which might hold historical significance to the approach of continuous learning across subjects.

HAPPY READING & LEARNING!

LECTOR HOUSE LLP
E-MAIL: lectorpublishing@gmail.com